conr

BIBLE STUDY GUIDE

Terror & Triumph

A Study of Revelation

Brian Harbour
Tom Howe
Ronny Marriott
Leigh Ann Powers

DISCOVER BELIEVE LIVE
BIBLE STUDY GUIDE

BaptistWayPress®
Dallas, Texas

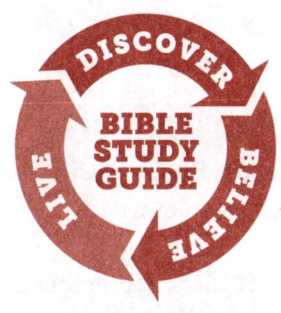

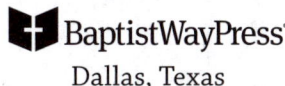

Terror & Triumph (A Study of Revelation)—Connect 360 Bible Study Guide

Copyright © 2016 by BAPTISTWAY PRESS®.
All rights reserved.
Printed in the United States of America.

No part of this book may be used or reproduced in any manner whatsoever without written permission except in the case of brief quotations. For information, contact BAPTISTWAY PRESS, Baptist General Convention of Texas, 7557 Rambler Road, Suite 1200, Dallas, TX 75231–2388.

BAPTISTWAY PRESS® is registered in U.S. Patent and Trademark Office.

Unless otherwise indicated, all Scripture quotations in "Introducing Terror & Triumph," and in lessons 1–7 are taken from the HOLY BIBLE, NEW INTERNATIONAL VERSION®. Copyright © 1973, 1978, 1984 Biblica. Used by permission of Zondervan. All rights reserved. NIV84 refers to this edition of the New International Version.

Unless otherwise indicated, all Scripture quotations in lessons 8–13 are from the 1995 update of the New American Standard Bible®, Copyright © The Lockman Foundation 1960, 1962, 1963, 1968, 1971, 1972, 1973, 1975, 1977, 1995. Used by permission. NASB refers to this edition of the New American Standard Bible®.

BAPTISTWAY PRESS® Leadership Team
Executive Director, Baptist General Convention of Texas: David Hardage
Director, Great Commission Team: Delvin Atchison
Publisher, BaptistWay Press®: Scott Stevens

Cover: Micah Kandros Design
Interior Design and Production: Desktop Miracles, Inc.
Printing: Data Reproductions Corporation

First edition: September 2016
ISBN–13: 978–1–938355–60–8

Introducing Connect 360

Welcome to Connect 360: All the Bible for All of Life from BaptistWay Press®. Connect 360 communicates our mission to connect people to God through his word. Our Bible study materials are designed to equip people everywhere to discover biblical truth, to believe the truth revealed in the Bible, and to live out this truth in their everyday lives. You see this represented in our "Discover-Believe-Live" logo which outlines this discipleship process.

Discover. Believe. Live.
A discipleship strategy focused on discovering, believing, and living out the truths of the Bible.

All the Bible for All of Life
Connect 360 exists to show all of the Bible as instrumental in revealing God's purpose and plan for life.

As evidenced in our tagline "All the Bible for All of Life," we believe God's word provides the wisdom and guidance we need to accomplish his will in the world. We also believe the Bible contains the truth we need to meet the challenges of life. We're excited to unveil this new look as we continue to provide trusted, biblical resources for you and your church.

Since 1999, BaptistWay Press® has published high quality Bible study resources, written by trusted Baptist authors. We commit to you to continue producing the same quality studies you expect from BaptistWay, written by Baptists who remain true to the biblical text and its interpretation. We believe all of the Bible, in its proper context, can teach and guide every part of our lives. Our mission is to help you and your church Discover the Truth of Scripture, Believe it, and Live it out every day. Welcome to Connect 360.

How to Make the Best Use of This Issue

Whether you're the teacher or a student—

1. Start early in the week before your class meets.
2. Overview the study. Review the table of contents and read the study introduction. Try to see how each lesson relates to the overall study.
3. Use your Bible to read and consider prayerfully the Scripture passages for the lesson. (You'll see that each writer has chosen a favorite translation for the lessons in this issue. You're free to use the Bible translation you prefer and compare it with the translation chosen for that unit, of course.)
4. After reading all the Scripture passages in your Bible, then read the writer's comments. The comments are intended to be an aid to your study of the Bible.
5. Read the small articles—"sidebars"—in each lesson. They are intended to provide additional, enrichment information and inspiration and to encourage thought and application.
6. Try to answer for yourself the questions included in each lesson. They're intended to encourage further thought and application, and they can also be used in the class session itself.

If you're the teacher—

Do all of the things just mentioned, of course. As you begin the study with your class, be sure to find a way to help your class know the date on which each lesson will be studied. Here are some suggestions to guide your lesson preparation:

How to Make the Best Use of This Issue

A. In the first session of the study, briefly overview the study by identifying for your class the date on which each lesson will be studied. Lead your class to write the date in the table of contents on page 9 and on the first page of each lesson.
- Make and post a chart that indicates the date on which each lesson will be studied.
- If all of your class has e-mail, send them an e-mail with the dates the lessons will be studied.
- Provide a bookmark with the lesson dates. You may want to include information about your church and then use the bookmark as an outreach tool, too. A model for a bookmark can be downloaded from www.baptistwaypress.org under the "Teacher Helps" menu.
- Develop a sticker with the lesson dates, and place it on the table of contents or on the back cover.

B. Get a copy of the *Teaching Guide*, a companion piece to this *Study Guide*. The *Teaching Guide* contains additional Bible comments plus two teaching plans. The teaching plans in the *Teaching Guide* are intended to provide practical, easy-to-use teaching suggestions that will work in your class.

C. After you've studied the Bible passage, the lesson comments, and other material, use the teaching suggestions in the *Teaching Guide* to help you develop your plan for leading your class in studying each lesson.

D. Teaching resource items for use as handouts are available free at www.baptistwaypress.org under the "Teacher Helps" tab.

E. Additional Bible study comments on the lessons are available online. Call 1-866-249-1799 or e-mail baptistway@texasbaptists.org to order the *Premium Commentary*. It is available only in electronic format (PDF) from our website, www.baptistwaypress.org. The price of these comments for the entire study is $5 per person. A church or class that participates in our advance order program for free shipping can receive the *Premium Commentary* free. Call 1-866-249-1799 or see www.baptistwaypress.org to purchase or for information on participating in our free shipping program for the next study.

F. Additional teaching plans are also available in electronic format (PDF) by calling 1–866–249–1799. The price of these additional teaching plans for the entire study is $5 per person. A church or class that participates in our advance order program for free shipping can receive the *Premium Teaching Plans* free. Call 1–866–249–1799 or see www.baptistwaypress.org for information on participating in our free shipping program for the next study.

G. Enjoy leading your class in discovering the meaning of the Scripture passages and in applying these passages to their lives.

Do you use a Kindle?

This Connect 360 *Bible Study Guide*, along with several other studies, is available in a Kindle edition. The easiest way to find these materials is to search for "BaptistWay" on your Kindle, or go to www.amazon.com/kindle and do a search for "BaptistWay." The Kindle edition can be studied not only on a Kindle but also on your smartphone or tablet using the Kindle app available free from amazon.com/kindle.

Writers for This *Study Guide*

Tom Howe wrote **lessons one through three**. Tom is the senior pastor of Birdville Baptist Church, Haltom City, Texas. Dr. Howe is a graduate of East Texas Baptist University (B.S.), Beeson Divinity School at Samford University (M. Div.), and Southwestern Baptist Theological Seminary (D. Min.).

Brian Harbour wrote **lessons four through seven**. Dr. Harbour has spent a lifetime teaching God's word and encouraging God's people. He served nine different churches in his forty-two years as a pastor of a local church. In his teaching ministry, he taught as a visiting professor or adjunct professor at Baylor University, George W. Truett Seminary, and Dallas Baptist University. In his writing ministry, he has authored seventeen books and for twenty-seven years produced a bi-monthly journal for pastors that included sermons, outlines, illustrations, and articles on preaching and leadership. He continues his ministry of encouragement through his non-profit organization, *SeminaryPLUS*.

Ronny Marriott wrote **lessons eight through ten**. Dr. Marriott is pastor of First Baptist Church, Temple, Texas. He holds the Doctor of Ministry degree from Southwestern Baptist Theological Seminary. Ronnie has written several studies for BaptistWay Press®.

Leigh Ann Powers wrote **lessons eleven through thirteen**. Leigh Ann is a freelance writer and mother of three from Winters, Texas. She is a graduate of Baylor University (B.S. Ed., 1998) and Southwestern Baptist Theological Seminary (M.Div., 2004). She attends First Baptist Winters, where her husband, Heath, serves as pastor. She blogs about faith, life, and family living at www.leighpowers.com.

Terror & Triumph
A Study of Revelation

How to Make the Best Use of This Issue   4
Writers for This Study Guide   7
Introducing Terror & Triumph (A Study of Revelation)   11

DATE OF STUDY

LESSON 1 _____ **The Revelation of Jesus Christ**
REVELATION 1   17

LESSON 2 _____ **Jesus' Letters to the Churches**
REVELATION 2:1–11; 3:1–6, 14–21   27

LESSON 3 _____ **The Lamb is Worthy**
REVELATION 4:1–6; 5:1–14   37

LESSON 4 _____ **Six Seals Opened**
REVELATION 6   47

LESSON 5 _____ **Intermission One: God's People Preserved**
REVELATION 7   57

LESSON 6 _____ **Trumpets of Judgment**
REVELATION 8; 9:1–6, 13–15, 20–21   67

LESSON 7 _____ **Intermission Two: Faithful Witnesses**
REVELATION 10:1–9; 11:1–15   77

LESSON 8 _____ **Saints vs. the Serpent**
REVELATION 12:1–6, 13–17; 13:1–4, 11–18   87

LESSON 9 _____ **The Forces of Evil Receive Judgment**
REVELATION 14:1–13   97

LESSON 10 _____ **Songs of Victory and Scenes of Destruction**
REVELATION 15:1–8; 16:12–21   107

LESSON 11 _____ **Babylon Falls**
REVELATION 17:1–6; 18:1–8   117

LESSON 12	**The Return of the King**	
	REVELATION 19:11–21; 20:1–10	127
LESSON 13	**A New Heaven and a New Earth**	
	REVELATION 21:1–8; 22:1–7, 16–17	137

Our Next New Study — 147

How to Order More Bible Study Materials — 149

Introducing

Terror & Triumph
A STUDY OF REVELATION

Approaching This Study of Revelation

The Revelation to John has long been regarded as a difficult book to understand, certainly by current readers but also by every generation of readers after the first. In the third century A.D., for example, Dionysius, the highly respected bishop of Alexandria, Egypt, sought to deal with a teaching about the millennium that was causing difficulty in that day. He did so by discouraging the literal interpretation of the book. According to the ancient church historian Eusebius, Dionysius also said of the Revelation, "I suppose that it is beyond my comprehension" and "it is too high for me to grasp."[1] So the struggle as to how to understand and interpret Revelation goes back quite a long way.

Certainly in our own day, the Book of Revelation continues to be a hot topic, even incendiary in nature. Perhaps more than any other book in the Bible, the interpretation of Revelation divides Christians, sometimes sharply.

If it is not seen as a book of division, Revelation certainly is seen as a book of mystery. What can we make of these images that often seem so bizarre? A starting place is to recognize the kind of book that Revelation is. Within the first four verses, we see this book described with names of two different kinds of literature and with a third kind of literature being implied.[2]

The first verse speaks of the book as a "revelation" (Revelation 1:1), a translation of the Greek word that is transliterated as *apocalypse*. The Book of Revelation thus shares some of the characteristics of other apocalyptic literature with which its readers would have been familiar. Apocalyptic literature tended to include such elements as these: (1) depictions of an intense struggle between good and evil; (2) a concern for the end time; (3) the use of symbols that often seemed unusual, such as animals representing people and with numbers having significance beyond simply the numbers themselves; (4) descriptions of cataclysmic, overwhelming events; (5) accounts of visions; (6) prominent roles for angels and demons. Even if you've never read the Book of Revelation completely, you likely see that these elements can be found quite readily within it.

In addition to being apocalyptic literature, Revelation 1:3 refers to the book as "prophecy" (see also Rev. 22:19). That is, this God-inspired writing told forth—and tells forth—God's message. This includes the forth telling of truth and the foretelling of future events.

Revelation 1:4 provides further information about the kind of literature included in this book. The form of this verse indicates that the Book of Revelation is also a letter "To the seven churches in the province of Asia" (1:4). This verse thus should serve rather pointedly to remind us that while the Revelation may speak to us, we are not its first intended readers. While some or all of the book may await fulfillment, we must remember as we try to understand the book that Revelation was written to people at a specific time and place in the first century A.D.

To what time and to what circumstances, though, was it written? Herschel Hobbs, the great Baptist statesman and Bible scholar, pointed out that two major dates have been suggested.[3] The first is in the 60s A.D., during the time of the Roman emperor Nero, and the second is in the 90s A.D., during the time of the Roman emperor Domitian. For Hobbs and many other scholars, the nod goes to the latter date as being most likely. Hobbs suggests A.D. 95 as being the most likely date of the writing of the Revelation.[4]

When we are in doubt as to the meaning of a passage in the Revelation, as we often are, and when opinions about interpreting a passage differ and differ sharply, as they often do, we can help ourselves if we will come back to this first touchstone, which is important no matter what the Bible book or passage is. That is, we should come back and ask what this passage most likely would have meant to its first readers. Only then should we allow ourselves to settle on making application to current events. Even then humility should move us to settle on such applications only lightly.

Here is an additional touchstone for interpreting Revelation. We will help ourselves in understanding this book that is so often hard to understand if we recognize that its teachings are more about God and God's Christ than about the future, whatever its details. The God of the Book of Revelation is a God who inspires awe. This God inspires awe in conquering his enemies.

Indeed, God's conquest of God's enemies occurs so easily that even when the scene is set for a great battle, what we see is not a battle but a quick victory (see 19:17–21). In fact, in the background of the entire Book of Revelation, even of the battle scenes, is the truth that the victory has been won already. The victory was won at the cross of Christ, the Lamb of God (5:6; 19:13), before which we can only stand in awe. Thus, the God of the Book of Revelation inspires awe in bringing redemption. Finally, when we get to the end of it all, we are awed to see a God who dwells with human beings and wipes the tears from their eyes (21:3–4).

The Book of Revelation in Our Day

The first readers of this book were dealing with great opposition and difficult, terrible circumstances. Maybe you are, too. If so, you may be in a better position to understand the book, for often the people who understand the Revelation best are those who are suffering for the sake of Christ. So, if you need encouragement, hope, and strength for dealing with difficult circumstances; that is what you will find in the Book of Revelation. In vivid pictures, this book reminds us that God will overcome everything that opposes God and threatens his people.

This is the second time BaptistWay Press® has produced a study on the Book of Revelation. For a complete listing of our studies see www.baptistwaypress.org.

TERROR & TRIUMPH: A STUDY OF REVELATION

Lesson 1	The Revelation of Jesus Christ	Revelation 1
Lesson 2	Jesus' Letters to the Churches	Revelation 2:1–11; 3:1–6, 14–21
Lesson 3	The Lamb is Worthy	Revelation 4:1–6; 5:1–14
Lesson 4	Six Seals Opened	Revelation 6
Lesson 5	Intermission One: God's People Preserved	Revelation 7
Lesson 6	Trumpets of Judgment	Revelation 8; 9:1–6, 13–15, 20–21
Lesson 7	Intermission Two: Faithful Witnesses	Revelation 10:1–9; 11:1–15
Lesson 8	Saints vs. the Serpent	Revelation 12:1–6, 13–17; 13:1–4, 11–18
Lesson 9	The Forces of Evil Receive Judgment	Revelation 14:1–13
Lesson 10	Songs of Victory and Scenes of Destruction	Revelation 15:1–8; 16:12–21
Lesson 11	Babylon Falls	Revelation 17:1–6; 18:1–8
Lesson 12	The Return of the King	Revelation 19:11–21; 20:1–10
Lesson 13	A New Heaven and a New Earth	Revelation 21:1–8; 22:1–7, 16–17

Additional Resources for Studying the *Revelation to John*[5]

Morris Ashcraft. "Revelation." *The Broadman Bible Commentary.* Volume 12. Nashville, Tennessee: Broadman Press, 1972.

William Barclay. *The Revelation of John.* Volumes 1 and 2. Second edition. Philadelphia: The Westminster Press, 1960.

G. K. Beale. *The Book of Revelation.* Grand Rapids, Michigan: Eerdmans, 1999.

G. R. Beasley-Murray. *The Book of Revelation.* New Century Bible. Greenwood, South Carolina: The Attic Press, 1974.

Joe Blair. *Introducing the New Testament.* Nashville: Broadman & Holman, 1994.

James L. Blevins. *Revelation.* Knox Preaching Guides. Atlanta: John Knox Press, 1984.

–––. *Revelation as Drama.* Nashville, Tennessee: Broadman Press, 1984.

Eugene Boring. *Revelation.* Interpretation: A Bible Commentary for Teaching and Preaching. Louisville: John Knox Press, 1989.

Herschel H. Hobbs. *The Cosmic Drama: An Exposition of the Book of Revelation.* Waco, Texas: Word Books, Publisher, 1971.

Craig S. Keener. *The NIV Application Commentary: Revelation.* Grand Rapids, Michigan: Zondervan Publishing House, 2000.

George Eldon Ladd. *A Commentary on the Revelation of John.* Grand Rapids, Michigan: William B. Eerdmans Publishing Company, 1972.

Edward A. McDowell. *The Meaning and Message of the Book of Revelation.* Nashville, Tennessee: Broadman Press, 1951.

Bruce M. Metzger. *Breaking the Code: Understanding the Book of Revelation.* Nashville, Tennessee: Abingdon Press, 1993.

John P. Newport. *The Lion and the Lamb: A Commentary on the Book of Revelation for Today.* Nashville, Tennessee: Broadman and Holman Publishers, 1986.

Eugene H. Peterson. *Reversed Thunder: The Revelation of John and the Praying Imagination.* San Francisco: HarperCollins, 1988.

Christopher C. Rowland. "The Book of Revelation." *The New Interpreter's Bible.* Volume XII. Nashville: Abingdon Press, 1998.

Ray Summers. *Worthy Is the Lamb.* Nashville, Tennessee: Broadman Press, 1951.

Merrill C. Tenney. *Interpreting Revelation.* Grand Rapids, Michigan: William B. Eerdmans Publishing, 1957.

Notes

1. Eusebius, *History of the Church*, VII.25. See http://www.newadvent.org/fathers/250107.htm, cited by G. R. Beasley-Murray, *The Book of Revelation*, New Century Bible (Greenwood, South Carolina: The Attic Press, 1974), 32–33.

2. Beasley-Murray, *Revelation*, 12. Dr. George Beasley-Murray, a Baptist, was an exceptionally gifted student and teacher of the New Testament, especially of Johannine literature and apocalyptic literature as well as of topics related to the kingdom of God.

3. Herschel H. Hobbs, *The Cosmic Drama: An Exposition of the Book of Revelation* (Waco, Texas: Word Books, Publisher, 1971), 11.

4. See John P. Newport, *The Lion and the Lamb: A Commentary on the Book of Revelation for Today* (Nashville, Tennessee: Broadman and Holman Publishers, 1986), 64–66. Beasley-Murray, *The Book of Revelation*, 37–38.

5. Listing a book does not imply full agreement by the writers or BAPTISTWAY PRESS® with all of its comments.

FOCAL TEXT
Revelation 1

BACKGROUND
Revelation 1

lesson 1

The Revelation of Jesus Christ

MAIN IDEA

No matter what comes, Jesus is in control.

QUESTION TO EXPLORE

What fears do you have for the future?

STUDY AIM

To summarize the meaning of John's vision and to affirm Christ's control of the future

QUICK READ

In the midst of a chaotic and uncertain world, we need a hope-filled and encouraging word. John's Revelation is such a word for his generation as well as ours.

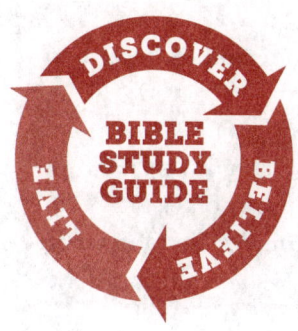

Introduction

Many Christians are hesitant to study the Book of Revelation based on confusion, fear of the text itself, or fear of the period it explains. Some Christians have chosen to ignore the book altogether, but John wrote it to strengthen and encourage believers living in uncertain times, not to lead them into fear or confusion.[1]

> ## Revelation 1
>
> **1** The revelation of Jesus Christ, which God gave him to show his servants what must soon take place. He made it known by sending his angel to his servant John, **2** who testifies to everything he saw—that is, the word of God and the testimony of Jesus Christ. **3** Blessed is the one who reads the words of this prophecy, and blessed are those who hear it and take to heart what is written in it, because the time is near.
>
> **4** John,
> To the seven churches in the province of Asia: Grace and peace to you from him who is, and who was, and who is to come, and from the seven spirits **5** before his throne, and from Jesus Christ, who is the faithful witness, the firstborn from the dead, and the ruler of the kings of the earth.
>
> **6** To him who loves us and has freed us from our sins by his blood, and has made us to be a kingdom and priests to serve his God and Father—to him be glory and power for ever and ever! Amen.
>
> **7** Look, he is coming with the clouds,
> and every eye will see him,
> even those who pierced him;
> and all the peoples of the earth will mourn because of him.
> So shall it be! Amen.
>
> **8** "I am the Alpha and the Omega," says the Lord God, "who is, and who was, and who is to come, the Almighty."
>
> **9** I, John, your brother and companion in the suffering and kingdom and patient endurance that are ours in Jesus, was on the island of Patmos because of the word of God and the testimony of Jesus. **10** On the Lord's Day I was in the Spirit, and I heard behind me a loud voice like a trumpet, **11** which said: "Write on a scroll what you see and send

Lesson 1: The Revelation of Jesus Christ

it to the seven churches: to Ephesus, Smyrna, Pergamum, Thyatira, Sardis, Philadelphia and Laodicea."

12 I turned around to see the voice that was speaking to me. And when I turned I saw seven golden lampstands, **13** and among the lampstands was someone "like a son of man," dressed in a robe reaching down to his feet and with a golden sash around his chest. **14** His head and hair were white like wool, as white as snow, and his eyes were like blazing fire. **15** His feet were like bronze glowing in a furnace, and his voice was like the sound of rushing waters. **16** In his right hand he held seven stars, and out of his mouth came a sharp double-edged sword. His face was like the sun shining in all its brilliance.

17 When I saw him, I fell at his feet as though dead. Then he placed his right hand on me and said: "Do not be afraid. I am the First and the Last. **18** I am the Living One; I was dead, and behold I am alive for ever and ever! And I hold the keys of death and Hades.

19 "Write, therefore, what you have seen, what is now and what will take place later. **20** The mystery of the seven stars that you saw in my right hand and of the seven golden lampstands is this: The seven stars are the angels of the seven churches, and the seven lampstands are the seven churches.

A Letter of Encouragement (1:1–2)

The Book of Revelation is not a cryptic code only broken by the highly intelligent or Bible scholars. It is a letter of encouragement and comfort for those living in difficult days, often because of their faith in Jesus. It is Jesus' final words of hope and victory. He holds the keys of death and Hades (Rev. 1:18), indicating that by his death, Jesus unlocked the prison doors of judgment. Therefore, we can trust that he is in complete control of the future, whatever that may be.

Like any letter, the Book of Revelation has an author, an audience, and a message. Understanding the author and the original audience helps us to understand the message more clearly today. The writer of Revelation was the

Apostle John, brother of James and son of Zebedee. He was one of the earliest disciples of Jesus, and he was exiled late in life for his Christian faith. Tradition holds that when John had the vision that would become the Book of Revelation, he was the sole survivor of Christ's twelve original disciples, living into his nineties.

John was the only disciple present at the death of Jesus, and his brother James was the first apostle martyred for his faith (Acts 12:1–2). One by one, John witnessed or received news of the death of each of the original disciples. He also witnessed the persecution of Christians under Emperor Nero (64–68 A.D.). At the end of his life, he was living in exile on the barren, rocky island of Patmos. John knew suffering (Rev. 1:9).

The opening phrase of this book could be translated "the revelation from Jesus Christ" as easily as "the revelation of Jesus Christ." Most scholars identify the syntax to mean this book is a revelation from Jesus, but it

Apocalypse

Apocalypse means "to uncover or reveal something hidden," hence the English name *Revelation*. In the Bible, the term refers to writing that uses symbolic language to describe how God will interact with humans in the near or distant future. The point of apocalyptic literature is to shed light on what God will do, not shroud it in darkness. The language is used to describe things in a general way that people of all generations can understand, at least to some degree, but that also solicits a strong response.

There are four common characteristics to all apocalyptic literature:

1. A struggle between God's goodness and ultimate evil (Satan or his followers)
2. A final predetermined victory by God
3. The use of imagery to emphatically describe the people, places, and activity of the end times
4. Rest and peace once the events conclude

Other books of the Bible that are apocalyptic, at least in part, include Daniel, Ezekiel, and Zechariah.

is also about him. This juxtaposition is an important actuality. Jesus did not directly author the other books of the Bible. Indeed, the Holy Spirit inspired the Scriptures, but the Book of Revelation is different. It contains the words of Jesus as revealed to John, who acted as one taking dictation for Jesus, as Jesus himself foretold end-of-time events. Jesus gave John, and consequently all Christians, a message of hope and encouragement in times of suffering and difficulty. Revelation is a much fuller response by Jesus to the disciples' question found in Matthew 24: "Tell us, when will these things happen, and what will be the sign of your coming, and of the end of the age?"

Revelation 1:4 reveals the original audience as the seven churches listed in chapters two and three. The message of Revelation first speaks to these churches in Asia Minor (modern-day Turkey) which was in the heart of the Christian world, located between Rome and Jerusalem. The region included major cities vital to military operations and commerce. However, the message of encouragement stretched far beyond this region since the book refers to the days leading up the return of Jesus and what will take place throughout the entire world and among all Christians.

A Message of Hope and Endurance (1:3–6)

The message of the Book of Revelation is one of hope and endurance. Instead of approaching the Scripture with fear and confusion, we should read it with an eye for what God will do in the end. In fact, we are considered "blessed" when we read it (1:3).

The first chapter of Revelation offers two main reasons for reading the book with optimistic enthusiasm. First, we are encouraged because of who Jesus is. He is everlasting (1:4, 8, 18), the firstborn from the dead (1:5, 18), and the ruler of the kings of the earth (1:5). Second, we are encouraged because of our calling as Christians. We, who have received grace and peace from God (1:4) and who have experienced his love and freedom (1:5), have been made to be a kingdom of priests to serve his God and Father (1:6).

Our calling is not to an easy, safe Christian experience. If it were, we would be confused and frustrated whenever life becomes difficult. There is no promise of a problem-free life as a Christian until Revelation 19–22, which reveals how the story ends. In the meantime, we are called to serve God's purposes. We are to advance his kingdom and to act as priests between him and those who do not know him. The Apostle Peter calls the church "a spiritual house to be a holy priesthood" (1 Peter 2:5).

Encouragement through Vivid Images (1:7–20)

Although the images and symbols depicted in the Book of Revelation can be confusing, they can also be understood in a meaningful way. The vibrant imagery evokes emotion and detailed explanation in much the same manner as today's pictures and video. Realizing that Jesus is the "he" of Revelation 1:7 (see also Rev. 2:18, "Son of God"), this verse reveals that "he is coming with the clouds" as a fulfillment of the prophecies found in Daniel 7:13 and Acts 1:9–11. Alpha is the first letter of the Greek alphabet and Omega is the last. By stating, "I am the Alpha and Omega" Jesus was communicating, "I am the beginning and the end," or "the total package." There is nothing greater than God, nothing before or after him.

Revelation 1:12–16 depicts images that can be easily demystified. The image of seven golden lampstands is reminiscent of the seven-branch lampstand found first in the tabernacle and then in the temple, and referenced in Zechariah 4:2, another apocalyptic text,. The Revelation passage does not describe these lampstands as connected or separated, but verse 20 states they represent the seven churches referenced in chapters two and three, which serve as light in darkness and the presence of God among his people.

Jesus is the "son of man" mentioned in Revelation 1:13. The description of a robe covering the feet of Jesus illustrates his importance. In Bible times, only dignitaries, priests, and royalty wore long robes. Commoners would have found long robes cumbersome for everyday work. Flowing robes may not sound extravagant today until we consider the dress of a modern bride with lace, a train, and an enormous amount of fabric. Such a dress is not for everyday activities. It is worn to set the bride apart as beautiful and special on her wedding day. Such will be the case of the long robe and golden sash Jesus will wear, depicting royalty, on the day described in Revelation 1:13.

The white hair described in 1:14 represents a collection of things: eternal age, wisdom, purity, and holiness. The blazing eyes portray one who is an

Lesson 1: *The Revelation of Jesus Christ*

all-perceiving, all-seeing, all-knowing, and perfect judge. (Revelation 19:12 also links these blazing eyes to Jesus, the rider on the white horse.) A modern way of saying "blazing eyes," is "eyes that pierce the soul." The bronze feet described in 1:15 represent strength and an unshakeable, immovable foundation, which describes Jesus' power.

The use of the words *voice* and *mouth* in verses 12 and 15 is central to this first chapter of Revelation. Jesus is the Word of God (John 1:1), and he created all things (John 1:1–3, Hebrews 1:1–3 and Colossians 1:16–17). The voice John heard sounded like a mighty rush of water. Anyone who has ever stood near a waterfall can relate to the deafening roar heard by John in his vision. The sword coming out of the mouth of Jesus is his penetrating, cutting, dividing, and revealing word from which there will be no escape (Heb. 4:12).

This Revelation 1 image of Jesus seems strange when painted on canvas because it is not intended to be an exact representation of him. The imagery speaks truth in the strongest language possible, setting up the language of the rest of the book. Revelation uses figurative language and graphic illustrations to describe events in both John's day and the distant future (1:19). John had no casual reaction to this appearance of Jesus. He immediately fell as though he were dead. Daniel had a similar response when he had a

Son of Man

Jesus' use of the title "Son of Man" is not a denial of his divinity, but an assertion of both his humanity and divinity. The title has two functions. As a human being, Jesus identified himself as part of humanity. As divine, Jesus pointed to his role of being the servant and deliverer of all of humanity. The title "Son of Man" is one of Jesus' favorite descriptions for himself; he used it more than eighty times throughout the Gospels when referring to himself, including Matthew 8:20, Mark 2:28, and Luke 21:27. The title is found 107 times in the Old Testament, mostly in Ezekiel and Daniel, and refers to the Messiah directly or indirectly in nearly all of its usages. Daniel 7:13–14 places the Son of Man with the Ancient of Days as the supreme eternal ruler. It is quite clear that the Son of Man in John's vision is King Jesus.

vision from God (Daniel 8:27). The responses of these two men challenge the modern notion of casually entering the presence of Jesus as though he is an ordinary buddy or friend. Remember that John was the closest friend Jesus had on earth, and yet John crumbled to the ground when he saw Jesus in his true holy essence.

Implications and Actions

Revelation is a book that some choose to ignore altogether while others read it as though they are trying to solve a cosmic puzzle. Neither approach is appropriate. Instead, we are encouraged to read the Book of Revelation as a blessing (1:3) for several reasons. We are blessed to have some general understanding of the end of time. With this knowledge, the church today may be better prepared for what lies ahead, just as the words of Jesus in Matthew 24–25 propelled Christians to escape Jerusalem when it fell in 70 A.D.. (Most of them were in Pella when the Romans destroyed Jerusalem.) Additionally, all Christians everywhere and at all times are encouraged by the message of Revelation when things are difficult. Our hope lies beyond our momentary suffering; it rests in the eternal Christ Jesus. Finally, although there are a lot of dark passages, Revelation is also filled with passages of victory, overcoming, and ultimate rest and peace. It reminds Christians everywhere that Jesus is in complete control, no matter what may happen. No other book in the Bible provides such a comprehensive view of ultimate triumph as Revelation.

Questions

1. Imagine you are John. After a lifetime of serving Jesus and enduring suffering and loss, you are now imprisoned on a remote island. How would you respond to seeing Jesus and learning of his vision?

2. Do you shy away from reading or studying the Book of Revelation? Why or why not?

3. Why do you think the Book of Revelation contains such descriptive language?

4. How does John's vision of Jesus apply to you?

Notes

1. Unless otherwise indicated, all Scripture quotations in lessons 1–7 are from the New International Version (1984 edition).

FOCAL TEXT
Revelation 2:1–11;
3:1–6, 14–21

BACKGROUND
Revelation 2–3

Jesus' Letters to the Churches

MAIN IDEA
Jesus commends the churches and calls them to repentance and faithfulness.

QUESTION TO EXPLORE
What does Christ want our church to do?

STUDY AIM
To outline the instructions in the letters and identify the implications for my church and my life

QUICK READ
Even if we are doing well in some areas of our faith, we need to constantly examine ourselves to be sure we are walking with the Lord in complete faithfulness.

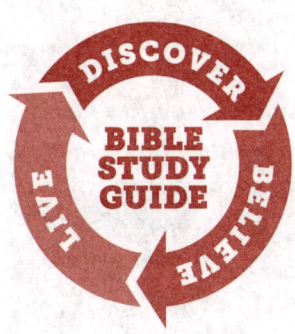

Introduction

The seven churches mentioned in Revelation were seven actual churches. They knew the Apostle John, and he knew them. Though the issues each church faced mirror those found in churches throughout history, it is best to begin studying this lesson with the knowledge that John was writing, first and foremost, to particular congregations dealing with personal problems. We can then extrapolate the messages from John to our situations.

The seven churches had unique combinations of good and bad qualities. Pergamum was a church which stood firm in persecution but lacked holiness, and also allowed false teachers in their midst. Its members held strong in their commitment to Christ, but failed at living moral lives.

Thyatira was a church that responded well to the call for action. It was strong in love, faith, service, and perseverance, but like Pergamum, Thyatira lacked holiness. Good deeds did not compensate for immorality. God is indeed interested in good works, but he also "searches hearts and minds" of all followers of Christ (Rev. 2:23).

The church of Philadelphia was a rare exception. It was faithful even under persecution, and Jesus said nothing critical of the Philadelphians. Instead, he expressed his love for them, said he would spare them from the hour of trial, and assured them he would come for them and bring ultimate victory.

Five of the seven churches were told to repent (2:5, 16, 22; 3:3, 19); Jesus assured the other two of receiving a crown of victory (2:10–11; 3:11–12).

Revelation 2:1–11

[1] "To the angel of the church in Ephesus write:
These are the words of him who holds the seven stars in his right hand and walks among the seven golden lampstands: [2] I know your deeds, your hard work and your perseverance. I know that you cannot tolerate wicked men, that you have tested those who claim to be apostles but are not, and have found them false. [3] You have persevered and have endured hardships for my name, and have not grown weary.

Lesson 2: *Jesus' Letters to the Churches*

⁴ Yet I hold this against you: You have forsaken your first love. ⁵ Remember the height from which you have fallen! Repent and do the things you did at first. If you do not repent, I will come to you and remove your lampstand from its place. ⁶ But you have this in your favor: You hate the practices of the Nicolaitans, which I also hate.

⁷ He who has an ear, let him hear what the Spirit says to the churches. To him who overcomes, I will give the right to eat from the tree of life, which is in the paradise of God.

⁸ "To the angel of the church in Smyrna write:

These are the words of him who is the First and the Last, who died and came to life again. ⁹ I know your afflictions and your poverty-yet you are rich! I know the slander of those who say they are Jews and are not, but are a synagogue of Satan. ¹⁰ Do not be afraid of what you are about to suffer. I tell you, the devil will put some of you in prison to test you, and you will suffer persecution for ten days. Be faithful, even to the point of death, and I will give you the crown of life.

¹¹ He who has an ear, let him hear what the Spirit says to the churches. He who overcomes will not be hurt at all by the second death.

Revelation 3:1–6, 14–21

¹ "To the angel of the church in Sardis write:

These are the words of him who holds the seven spirits of God and the seven stars. I know your deeds; you have a reputation of being alive, but you are dead. ² Wake up! Strengthen what remains and is about to die, for I have not found your deeds complete in the sight of my God. ³ Remember, therefore, what you have received and heard; obey it, and repent. But if you do not wake up, I will come like a thief, and you will not know at what time I will come to you.

⁴ Yet you have a few people in Sardis who have not soiled their clothes. They will walk with me, dressed in white, for they are worthy. ⁵ He who overcomes will, like them, be dressed in white. I will never blot out his name from the book of life, but will acknowledge his name before my Father and his angels. ⁶ He who has an ear, let him hear what the Spirit says to the churches.

14 "To the angel of the church in Laodicea write:

These are the words of the Amen, the faithful and true witness, the ruler of God's creation. **15** I know your deeds, that you are neither cold nor hot. I wish you were either one or the other! **16** So, because you are lukewarm—neither hot nor cold—I am about to spit you out of my mouth. **17** You say, 'I am rich; I have acquired wealth and do not need a thing.' But you do not realize that you are wretched, pitiful, poor, blind and naked. **18** I counsel you to buy from me gold refined in the fire, so you can become rich; and white clothes to wear, so you can cover your shameful nakedness; and salve to put on your eyes, so you can see.

19 Those whom I love I rebuke and discipline. So be earnest, and repent. **20** Here I am! I stand at the door and knock. If anyone hears my voice and opens the door, I will come in and eat with him, and he with me.

21 To him who overcomes, I will give the right to sit with me on my throne, just as I overcame and sat down with my Father on his throne.

Loveless Faith (2:1–7)

Ephesus was a large, powerful, beautiful, wealthy, and influential city. It was a center of banking and commerce, and it housed the famous Temple of Artemis, known as Diana in Rome. She was the goddess of fertility, youth, and beauty. Ephesus was a central, vibrant seaport and a key city on the overland route. Paul, Timothy, and John all served as pastors in the church of Ephesus, and with such strong theological training, its people correctly dealt with false prophets. The Nicolaitans taught a mixed message of immorality and idolatry—and possibly the pagan practices of other religions. The Ephesians stood firm in their faith even in such a diverse community. They worked hard, served well, and did not fall into the immorality that plagued many of the surrounding churches.

The chief accusation against the Ephesians was they had forsaken their first love (2:4). They knew Scripture well and lived exemplary lives, yet perhaps their knowledge and morality became the totality of their faith. They had forgotten Jesus' words that the great commandments were to "Love the Lord your God with all your heart and with all your soul and with all your mind" and to "Love your neighbor as yourself" (Matthew 22: 37, 39).

There are many aspects of the Christian walk. We certainly need to apply correct theology. We must stand up for what we believe. We must walk in obedience. We must serve others, as well as the kingdom of God, but we must never have a loveless faith. Paul wrote that if we are eloquent speakers, masters of the Bible, faithful warriors, selfless servants, or even martyrs, but are loveless, then we gain nothing (1 Corinthians 13:1–3).

Our first love is Jesus. We must cherish this relationship and adore him. As important as our identity and how we think and live are, we must not fail to love in the right way! Because of its lack of love, Ephesus ran the risk of losing its lampstand, which represented the crumbling of the church; so too will our churches crumble if we lose the love that binds us to one another and to God.

Persecuted Faith (2:8–11)

Smyrna was a beautiful city built on the rising slope of Mount Pagus. Every detail was planned to aesthetic perfection to emphasize its beauty—from the city's perfectly situated harbor to its stunning mountainside. The city's amenities were modern and fashionable. In such a setting, Smyrna was known for two things: splendor and suffering. The church had experienced harassment and would later endure severe persecution. John predicted as much in his letter (2:8–11). It is likely one of John's own pupils, Polycarp, either carried the letter to Smyrna or was the pastor of the church when the letter was read. Polycarp would rise to be one the greatest of the early church fathers, only to be executed in Smyrna for his faith late in life. It appears the church in Smyrna wore a target for harassment and oppression. Yet, they received the great assurance of life and victory.

There have been many throughout Christian history who have endured hardship and persecution for their faith. Indeed, there are many today experiencing intimidation, discrimination, mistreatment, and even torture for their faith. Christians around the world are aware of political, social, and religious infringements and difficulties. These challenges are on the rise

> ## Repent
>
> The Greek word for repent is *metanoeo,* which is a combination of two words, *meta* and *noeo*. *Meta* means "against, with, or after." *Noeo* means "to consider, to comprehend or to understand;" it is the root word of "to know" or "knowledge." *Metanoeo* means all of the following wrapped in one: "with understanding, after further consideration, and against my former way of thinking." Repentance is the process of mental deliberation resulting in a sound understanding or agreement to a new and changed reality, changing from a negative position to a positive one.
>
> In English, the definition of *repentance* is "to change one's mind," but it implies a change of action as well. Repentance is more than just saying, "I'm sorry" and then expecting everything to return to normal. It is a complete overhaul of mind and action. Jesus warned the seven churches mentioned in the Book of Revelation to change their ways or face dire consequences. His warning applies to Christians in any place and at any time.

in a destabilizing world. The message to Smyrna is as relevant now as ever to Christians enduring suffering: Do not be afraid! Be strong! You will be victorious!

This letter to Smyrna opposes "easy-believe" Christianity and "name-it-and-claim-it" prosperity theology. There is no biblical promise of a problem-free life or a problem-free church just because we belong to Jesus Christ. In fact, Jesus warned his followers the world would hate the church and mistreat it (John 15:18–16:3).

Borrowed Faith (3:1–6)

Sardis was a city with a long and glorious history. It had been a city of great wealth because of the gold found in the region. (It is the setting for the story of King Midas with the golden touch.) The city also had a large citadel sitting on high slopes, which appeared impregnable. However, the occupying army was overconfident in its defenses, which led to defeat on more than

Lesson 2: Jesus' Letters to the Churches

one occasion. The city's long religious history included Jews from early on. Many scholars believe Sardis was the city of Sepharad, from which came many Jewish exiles (Obadiah 1:20). By the time of the Roman occupation, the city's citadel was much less significant. It was one-third its original size, and the gold mines were empty. An earthquake in 17 A.D. further eroded the value of Sardis. The city was a shadow of its glory days.

Jesus' accusations against the church in Sardis echoed its military and economic experience. They were living on a long-held *reputation* of faith, which was a shadow of its former days. They were trying to live on a borrowed faith, whether it was borrowed from their previous days or from their two closest neighbors, Smyrna and Ephesus, which were commended by the Lord. Jesus warned the church in Sardis that reputation alone was not enough.

"Wake up!" was the urgent command Jesus had for this city. They had the reputation of being alive, but he knew they were spiritually dead. Another way to say it is, "come alive" or "watch out!" Borrowed faith may also be referred to as "holdover faith," held over from a previous time or experience in one's life, or even possibly from a previous generation. It is not enough that one's grandfather was a preacher, or one's mother was a saintly woman. Each person must have genuine faith or risk the judgment issued upon Sardis, but the one who is faithful and victorious will never be blotted out from the book of life (Rev. 3:5).

Self-sufficient Faith (3:14–21)

Laodicea was a rich city that had little need for assistance from Rome. Whereas Ephesus, Smyrna, and Pergamum were coastal cities with strong connections to Rome and its way of life, Laodicea was a city located inland without easy connection to Rome or other major trade cities. Situated in a fertile valley under high mountains, Laodicea (modern-day Panukkale in Turkey) had bright-white mineral deposits at its peak, which gave the illusion of perpetual snow.

Laodicea had soil that was excellent for crops, and the city featured a banking center, as well as a medical facility; perhaps due to nearby mineral

> ## I Stand at the Door and Knock
>
> Revelation 3:20, "Here I am! I stand at the door and knock," is often used in church invitations or personal evangelism as a prompt for someone to consider giving their life to Christ. Although such imagery seems valid, remember that the original readers of this verse were people who were already Christians, the Laodiceans. Rather than a call to salvation, John used this phrase to call lukewarm Christians back to a vibrant life in Jesus.

deposits. The city was predominantly self-sufficient; however, two nearby cities, Colossae and Hierapolis, had distinct and unique advantages. Colossae was near enough to its mountain to access pure water from the run-off of cold, melted snow. Hierapolis had hot, mineral-laced springs ideal for medicinal baths. Laodicea had neither the fresh, cold, tasty water of Colossae, nor the steamy medicinal water of Hierapolis. Its mineral-laced, tepid water, which was neither refreshingly cold nor beneficially hot, left a bad taste in the mouth of anyone who drank it.

Laodicea's self-sufficiency as a city bled over into its church, which did not solicit help from anyone, including God. It saw itself as wealthy and capable of taking care of its needs. However, spiritual self-sufficiency is the opposite of faith. It removes the need for God and replaces him with self, the very act that led to Satan's downfall. Jesus compared the faith of the Laodicieans to that of their water, neither refreshing nor beneficial, neither cold nor hot. Their faith was tepid and of little use. John graphically writes that God will spit them out like inferior, offensive water.

Implications and Actions

It is not easy to face our faults. Like many churches today, the seven churches depicted in the Book of Revelation had their share of good and bad qualities. They serve as reminders to us to diligently discover our faults, repent of them, and grow in Christ. In a challenging world, we need correct theology, sound morality, a servant's heart, and a firm stance amidst persecution. We also must maintain a dependent faith and a constant love for God and his

Lesson 2: *Jesus' Letters to the Churches*

people. We tend to be strong in one or two spiritual disciplines, but we may lack in others. We must focus on strengthening our weak areas as individual Christians, and as an entire church. Jesus warned of grave consequences for those who do not meet his expectations. We should heed his warning, repent, and return to him with pure hearts, souls, and minds.

Questions

1. Can you give an illustration of a church that knows all the right things, but demonstrates a loveless faith? How would you describe the faith of your church?

2. Many Christians face persecution throughout the world—ranging from discrimination, ridicule, arrest, and torture to execution. What hope do you find in Revelation 2:10 and 3:11–12? What can you do to encourage those facing persecution?

3. What dangers are related to having a borrowed faith, whether it is from another person or the past?

4. Describe self-sufficient faith. What are the detriments of such a faith?

FOCAL TEXT
Revelation 4:1–7; 5

BACKGROUND
Revelation 4–5

lesson 3

The Lamb is Worthy

MAIN IDEA
Scenes of heavenly worship reveal Jesus as the source of the meaning of history and life itself.

QUESTION TO EXPLORE
Where can I find the meaning of history and of my life?

STUDY AIM
To describe the role of Christ in providing meaning to history and to my life

QUICK READ
John used amazing imagery to depict a heavenly scene with Jesus as the center of our meaning and worship.

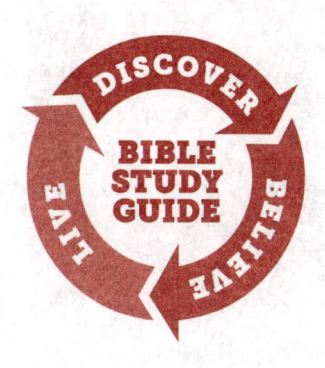

Introduction

Chapters 4 and 5 of the Book of Revelation link Jesus' initial message to the churches with the judgment foretold in chapters 6–18. They are reassuring chapters, written to remind readers that Jesus has all authority, power, and control. He can handle whatever may be coming. He is the center of worship and meaning in life.

Revelation 4:1–7

1 After this I looked, and there before me was a door standing open in heaven. And the voice I had first heard speaking to me like a trumpet said, "Come up here, and I will show you what must take place after this." **2** At once I was in the Spirit, and there before me was a throne in heaven with someone sitting on it. **3** And the one who sat there had the appearance of jasper and carnelian. A rainbow, resembling an emerald, encircled the throne. **4** Surrounding the throne were twenty-four other thrones, and seated on them were twenty-four elders. They were dressed in white and had crowns of gold on their heads. **5** From the throne came flashes of lightning, rumblings and peals of thunder. Before the throne, seven lamps were blazing. These are the seven spirits of God. **6** Also before the throne there was what looked like a sea of glass, clear as crystal.

7 In the center, around the throne, were four living creatures, and they were covered with eyes, in front and in back. The first living creature was like a lion, the second was like an ox, the third had a face like a man, the fourth was like a flying eagle.

Revelation 5

1 Then I saw in the right hand of him who sat on the throne a scroll with writing on both sides and sealed with seven seals. **2** And I saw a mighty angel proclaiming in a loud voice, "Who is worthy to break the seals and open the scroll?" **3** But no one in heaven or on earth or under the earth could open the scroll or even look inside it. **4** I wept and wept because no one was found who was worthy to open the scroll or look inside. **5** Then one of the elders said to me, "Do not weep! See, the Lion of the tribe of Judah, the Root of David, has triumphed. He is able to open the scroll and its seven seals."

6 Then I saw a Lamb, looking as if it had been slain, standing in the center of the throne, encircled by the four living creatures and the elders. He had seven horns and seven eyes, which are the seven spirits of God sent out into all the earth. **7** He came and took the scroll from the right hand of him who sat on the throne. **8** And when he had taken it, the four living creatures and the twenty-four elders fell down before the Lamb. Each one had a harp and they were holding golden bowls full of incense, which are the prayers of the saints. **9** And they sang a new song:

> "You are worthy to take the scroll
>   and to open its seals,
> because you were slain,
> and with your blood you purchased men for God from every
>   tribe and language and people and nation.
> **10** You have made them to be a kingdom and priests to serve
>   our God, and they will reign on the earth."

11 Then I looked and heard the voice of many angels, numbering thousands upon thousands, and ten thousand times ten thousand. They encircled the throne and the living creatures and the elders. **12** In a loud voice they sang:

> "Worthy is the Lamb, who was slain,
>   to receive power and wealth and wisdom and strength and
>   honor and glory and praise!"

13 Then I heard every creature in heaven and on earth and under the earth and on the sea, and all that is in them, singing:

> "To him who sits on the throne and to the Lamb be praise and
>   honor and glory and power,
> for ever and ever!"

14 The four living creatures said, "Amen," and the elders fell down and worshiped.

A Throne in Heaven (4:1–7)

In Revelation 4:1, the phrase "after this," is used twice, prompting the question, *After what?* It is an overreaction to translate this as anything other than *after the first part of the vision*, in which John was given the letters to the churches. John was told to "Come up here," which was his calling to take a place in the middle of an incredible scene. Most scholars understand "in the Spirit" as referring to John being caught up in an ecstatic trance into the realms of heaven itself, much like Paul in 2 Corinthians 12:1–6. The open door signified the ease of access that John had in his vision. The entire astonishing sight is metaphorical.

The one who sat on the throne had the appearance of jasper and ruby, which are brilliant gemstones (Rev. 4:3). Ruby is a bloodred stone. Jasper is a translucent, iridescent stone much like a diamond. It can be a single color or multi-colored, and produces a prism-like appearance, perhaps like a modern-day hologram. That colorful description, along with "a rainbow, resembling an emerald, encircled the throne," indicated a dazzling aura before John, a scene of ultimate visual beauty whose magnificence was unequaled.

The Number Seven

The Bible uses the number "seven" to symbolize completion, especially the completed work of God. God used seven days to finish creation. There were seven Jewish holidays and seven sets of seven years to arrive at the year of Jubilee (for a total of 49 years—see Leviticus 25:8–13). The Book of Revelation features a series of sevens: seven lampstands, spirits, churches, horns, eyes, seals, trumpets, and bowls. It helps to avoid confusion by realizing that each "seven" symbolizes God's completed plan. John records that the Lamb had seven horns and seven eyes (Rev. 5:6). Horns represent power and eyes represent perception and vision, meaning that the Lamb had God's full measure of power and insight. There is no attempt to provide a literal description of what Jesus looks like in heaven. The seven eyes, which become the seven spirits (also translated as sevenfold Spirit), represent the fullness of God's presence in the Holy Spirit as extending from the Lamb. It is unnecessary to read more into the number seven than God's completed work.

Lesson 3: The Lamb is Worthy

In John's vision, twenty-four elders wearing white attire and gold crowns surrounded the throne (4:1). There are three primary theories regarding the identity of these elders. The first is that the elders represent a council of angelic or heavenly beings. This theory is the least plausible interpretation since no validation for such a council exists elsewhere in Scripture. Neither is there evidence of anyone except human saints wearing white clothing and crowns; therefore, the elders must certainly be human.

The second theory interprets the twenty-four elders as a generic number which doubles the number twelve, which is considered God's perfect number, symbolizing his power and authority. In this context, the elders would've represented the entire kingdom of creation, gathering around Jesus in worship and submission.

The last and most reasonable explanation is that the twenty-four elders represent the combination of the twelve tribes of Israel joined with the twelve apostles, to signify the entire breadth of the people of God. In this view, the twenty-four elders could be symbolic, or actual individuals. (The latter premise presents a set of difficulties. If the council does indeed include the twelve apostles, then it would make sense that the lone surviving apostle, John, would be with the other apostles.) The white attire worn by the elders symbolized Christ's extended righteousness, and the crowns illustrate the apostles' authority under Jesus.

The flashes of lightning and peals of thunder emphasize God's power and magnificence, and the crystal sea radiated his brilliant appearance (4:5–6). John described a vision that would completely overwhelm the senses: sight, sound, and smell. (Revelation 5:8 describes the elders holding bowls of incense and 8:2–5 reiterates the assault on the senses.)

John saw four living creatures positioned between the throne and the elders. These creatures represented the fullness of creation (4:6–7). The lion was a picture of the noblest of creatures. The ox stood for strength. The man represented wisdom, and the eagle symbolized the swiftest creatures. (These creatures also appear in Ezekiel 1 and 10.) All four creatures had six wings (like angels) and many eyes, which were all-seeing and never-resting, constantly worshipping and praising God in his throne room.

A Worthy Lamb (5:1–7)

Chapter five is a continuation of the throne room vision with the introduction of a scroll. The Greek word for "scroll" is *biblion,* the derivative word for *Bible*. It is the absolute authoritative word of God, which holds the judgment to come. In John's vision, the one on the throne held a sealed scroll, which when opened would reveal the final act of creation. A mighty angel asked, "Who is worthy to break the seals and open the scroll?" and thus able to usher in the final era of history (5:1–2).

In verse 6, John made a unique choice for the word *Lamb* introduced in this passage. Instead of the Greek word *amnos,* which is the standard term for a sacrificial lamb, he described this Lamb as *arnion,* which is the Greek word for a young lamb. This imagery depicts a child (son), instead of an adult, making it appear unlikely that he would be fit for authority. Furthermore, the Lamb looked "as if it had been slain," adding to the diminutive status.

John was overwhelmed by the emotion of the moment, but an elder assured him of the Lamb's ability to open the scroll and bring about its fulfillment. The entire scene ascribes complete and unique authority to the Lamb; only he is worthy to open the scroll. Verse five makes it clear that Jesus is the Lamb. He is the Lion of Judah who fulfills Genesis 49:10, "The scepter will not depart from Judah, nor the ruler's staff from between his feet, until he comes to whom it belongs and the obedience of the nations is his." Jesus is also the Root of David, receiving the complete authority, power, and worth of the Lord (Isaiah 11).

> ## An Analysis of Worship
>
> Critically examine your state of mind and heart in how you worship God. Recall the worship descriptions of Revelation 4 and 5. How do they compare to your style of worship? Will thinking about the worship in Revelation affect how you praise God today? Has your worship recently focused more on you and your needs than on the Lord and who he is? Today, seek to worship God as described in Revelation 5, the way we all will respond when in the actual presence of the Lamb.

Lesson 3: *The Lamb is Worthy*

This commonality links Revelation 5:5 to Isaiah 11:1–2, which lists the seven spirits that come to rest on the root of Jesse, the father of David: the Spirit of the Lord, wisdom, understanding, counsel, power, knowledge, and fear. Considering that John made a connection to Old Testament messianic prophecies (Daniel, Ezekiel, Zechariah, Genesis), it makes sense he linked the Lamb to the one who received the sevenfold Spirit of the Lord (Rev. 3:1), especially noting that he immediately referenced the seven spirits.

Hymns of Praise (5:8–14)

In Revelation 5:8–14, the Lamb is the object of worship of the four living creatures and the twenty-four elders. This focus means all creation, as well as the people of God (Old and New Testament), will recognize him as worthy of worship and praise.

This Scripture passage features three hymns of praise. The first hymn, found in verses 9–10, is sung by the four living creatures and the twenty-four elders in the midst of the prayers of the saints and is a hymn of worth and ability. The Lamb can do what no one else can. He can open the scrolls. His ability comes from having been slain and then triumphant over death (verses 5 and 6). The blood of the Lamb is the purchase price for all who would believe and who have been enabled to rule with Jesus. We sing today because of the work of salvation Jesus accomplished for us. He saved us from sin and its consequence, but he also saved us to something, namely to become a kingdom of priests to serve our God and to reign on earth.

The choir is enlarged in verses 11–12 to include tens of thousands of angels who join the living creatures and the elders. This song is a hymn of character. Not only is Jesus able to open the scrolls, but he is also the object of all worship. With all humanity and the angels recognizing the worth of the Lamb, he is praised to the highest degree. We must praise Jesus for more than just what he has done for us (as wonderful as that is). We must praise him for who he is.

Finally, the last song represents a hymn of eternal boundlessness (verse 13). All creatures everywhere join the chorus. No one remains who does not sing the everlasting praise of Jesus. This hymn means all honor, glory, and power are his for all of eternity. With the final "Amen," the creatures and elders bow and worship to indicate only the Lamb deserves praise. Jesus has supreme power and authority. Nothing in the scrolls yet to be fulfilled on earth is outside of the hands of Jesus (literally). Nothing will overcome him. He is in complete control now and forever.

What great comfort for the followers of Jesus! Not only is he in complete control, but he empowers us to join him in service and authority. The next few chapters of the Book of Revelation will speak of troublesome events, but understanding the power and worth of Jesus provides eternal confidence and assurance for all believers. This hope is true for the end of time, as well as for the time in which we live. Let us find our hope and confidence in Jesus Christ, the Lamb who was slain, but who is worthy to receive all power, wealth, wisdom, strength, honor, glory, and praise!

Implications and Actions

Revelation is a beautiful book filled with hope and praise. Given its complexities, there are many different levels of understanding; however, the heart of the book, in general, and chapters four and five, in particular, reveal that Jesus holds all of life together. We worship him because of who he is and what he has done. One day, all creation will worship him. He died to give us eternal life, as well as meaning and purpose for our lives. We will sing the hymns of praise for eternity, so let us not become distracted from wholeheartedly worshipping him in this world now!

Questions

1. How would you respond if you were called to "come up here" and then saw what John saw?

Lesson 3: *The Lamb is Worthy* 45

2. Compare Revelation 4:1–6 with Isaiah 6:1–8. What are the similarities and differences?

3. Why do you think John wept in Revelation 5:4?

4. Imagine the expanding choir of Revelation 5—every creature in heaven, on earth, and even under the earth and the sea singing and worshipping Jesus. How do you think you will feel at that moment?

5. When life seems to spin out of control, how does the knowledge that Jesus holds all aspects of your life in his hands reassure you? Who do you know who needs this reassurance?

FOCAL TEXT
Revelation 6

BACKGROUND
Revelation 6

lesson 4
Six Seals Opened

MAIN IDEA
As God orchestrates the end of time, he will bring severe judgments.

QUESTION TO EXPLORE
Why must judgment come?

STUDY AIM
To explain the meaning of the six seals and identify implications for my life today

QUICK READ
God will ultimately display his righteousness as he unleashes his judgment on the unrighteous and as he brings redemption to his faithful people.

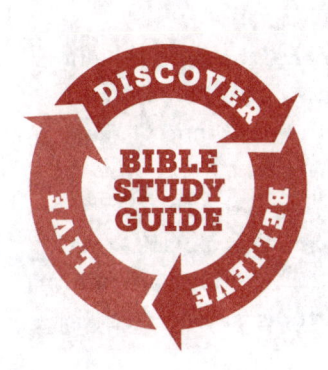

Introduction

The first time he orchestrated a break-in, he got away with it. He was too impatient to wait until after the weekend to receive the results of his final exams. He knew he had done well at Duke Law School, but he wanted to discover if he landed at the top of his class. He and his team pulled off the clandestine dean's office break-in flawlessly. He was not so fortunate later in life when he orchestrated another break-in to discover his opponent's election strategy. He was confident he would win the election but wanted to win by a landslide and crush his opponent. Consequently, he authorized a clandestine operation to break into the Democratic National Committee Headquarters at the Watergate Hotel. This time, Richard Nixon did not get away with it. This break-in cost him the presidency. He discovered a fundamental principle of life: eventually we suffer the consequences of unwise choices.

At the time John wrote the Book of Revelation, the Roman Empire appeared impregnable and unstoppable. The oppressive Roman rulers wreaked havoc on all who opposed them, especially Christians. John used the image of the Lamb opening seven seals to assure Christians that Rome would eventually suffer the consequences of her oppressive behavior.

Revelation 6

1 I watched as the Lamb opened the first of the seven seals. Then I heard one of the four living creatures say in a voice like thunder, "Come!" **2** I looked, and there before me was a white horse! Its rider held a bow, and he was given a crown, and he rode out as a conqueror bent on conquest.

3 When the Lamb opened the second seal, I heard the second living creature say, "Come!" **4** Then another horse came out, a fiery red one. Its rider was given power to take peace from the earth and to make men slay each other. To him was given a large sword.

5 When the Lamb opened the third seal, I heard the third living creature say, "Come!" I looked, and there before me was a black horse! Its rider was holding a pair of scales in his hand. **6** Then I heard what sounded like a voice among the four living creatures, saying, "A quart

> of wheat for a day's wages, and three quarts of barley for a day's wages, and do not damage the oil and the wine!"
>
> **7** When the Lamb opened the fourth seal, I heard the voice of the fourth living creature say, "Come!" **8** I looked, and there before me was a pale horse! Its rider was named Death, and Hades was following close behind him. They were given power over a fourth of the earth to kill by sword, famine and plague, and by the wild beasts of the earth.
>
> **9** When he opened the fifth seal, I saw under the altar the souls of those who had been slain because of the word of God and the testimony they had maintained. **10** They called out in a loud voice, "How long, Sovereign Lord, holy and true, until you judge the inhabitants of the earth and avenge our blood?" **11** Then each of them was given a white robe, and they were told to wait a little longer, until the number of their fellow servants and brothers who were to be killed as they had been was completed.
>
> **12** I watched as he opened the sixth seal. There was a great earthquake. The sun turned black like sackcloth made of goat hair, the whole moon turned blood red, **13** and the stars in the sky fell to earth, as late figs drop from a fig tree when shaken by a strong wind. **14** The sky receded like a scroll, rolling up, and every mountain and island was removed from its place.
>
> **15** Then the kings of the earth, the princes, the generals, the rich, the mighty, and every slave and every free man hid in caves and among the rocks of the mountains. **16** They called to the mountains and the rocks, "Fall on us and hide us from the face of him who sits on the throne and from the wrath of the Lamb! **17** For the great day of their wrath has come, and who can stand?"

The Scroll, the Seals, and the Lamb (6:1a)

The text for this lesson occupies a central place in the vision that begins in Revelation 4:1 and concludes with the opening of the seventh seal in 8:1–5. The one who sat on the throne in John's vision held in his hand a scroll that had writing on both sides of the parchment, implying that this scroll contained many words.

Some suggest this scroll symbolizes God's testament describing the inheritance that will come to those who give their allegiance to him. Others believe the scroll announces the judgment that will fall on earth. The context seems to support the latter position. When the seals break, we see more and more clearly the judgment that will come on those who oppose God's kingdom.

The scroll was "sealed with seven seals" (5:1). In the ancient world, the seal on a document guaranteed its authenticity and provided protection against tampering. The seven seals on the scroll in John's vision affirm this document as a genuine message from God and that it was protected from distortion. However, the seals that authenticated and protected the document also posed a problem. Who could break the seven seals and reveal the contents of the scroll? An angel voiced that dilemma in Revelation 5:2, and at first no one in the entire universe appeared to be able to open the scroll. Consequently, John wept tears of disappointment and dismay. If the seals could not be broken, God's plan could not be known. Even worse, God's plan could not be implemented.

But then one of the elders interrupted John's lament and announced the good news of one worthy to break the seals and open the scroll: "the Lion of the tribe of Judah, the Root of David" (5:5). The context makes it clear that John used these terms to describe the Lamb of God (5:6). In John's vision, the Lamb stepped forward and took the scroll from the hand of the one seated on the throne. After taking the scroll, the Lamb broke the seals and executed the plan of God. What no one else in the universe was worthy to do, the Lamb could accomplish.

The Method of Judgment (6:1b–8)

With the breaking of each of the successive seals, we see the dimensions of God's judgment unfold. Notice that the judgment of God unleashed by the opening of the seals is the first of three judgments John identified: the seals (6:1–8:5), the trumpets (8:6–21, 11:15), and the bowls (16:1–21). In each of these judgments, John described several dimensions of judgment. Notice that God will use human instruments, natural disasters on Earth, and cosmic disasters to implement these judgments.

As the Lamb broke the first four seals, each of "the four living creatures" in turn summoned John to "Come" (6:1; 6:3; 6:5; 6:7). John introduced these four living creatures in Revelation 4:6. Who are these four living creatures? Most commentators assert that the four living creatures represent all creation. The lion represents wild animal life, the calf represents domestic animal life, the man represents human life, and the eagle represents bird life, each creature being the chief of its class. Perhaps John's primary goal was not to identify what the four creatures represent but to spotlight their actions. These creatures reflected their adoration of God on his throne through a never-ending doxology of praise to him (4:8). In the text for this lesson, they participated in the unfolding judgment of God. As each of the first four seals broke, they called out the components of God's judgment with a resolute, "Come!"

The first four seals represent the different instruments God will use to bring judgment on the Roman Empire. Each of these first four judgments involves a person riding a horse. Most commentators connect this imagery with the prophecy in Zechariah 1:8–17 in which horses and riders patrol the earth to discern the conditions that prevail. John's horses and riders in Revelation 6 already know the conditions that prevail and consequently carry out God's judgment against the unrighteous.

The white horse mounted by a rider with a bow represents a conquering invader (6:1–2). The red horse empowered to "take peace from the earth" represents war, the bloody means the conquering invaders will use to carry out God's judgment (6:3–4). The black horse represents famine, which often followed war in the ancient world (6:5–6). The pale horse represents plagues that, like famine, often accompany war and cover humanity with the cloak of death (6:7–8). God will use these evil forces to punish the world for its sin.

The Reason for Judgment (6:9–16a)

With the opening of the fifth seal, John changed his focus from the method of judgment, described in the aftermath of the breaking of the first four seals, to the reason for judgment (6:9–11). Saints who had been martyred by Emperor Domitian called for God's justice. John pulled his imagery from the temple setting. In the temple, a small trough placed under the altar caught the blood of sacrificed animals. In his vision, John saw in this trough "the souls of those who had been slain" (6:9).

The white robe given to those who have died for their faith in Christ signifies that God will alter their status from suffering martyrs to righteous saints. This final reckoning will come after the number of deaths "was completed" (6:11). John's vision does not imply that a certain number of saints must die as martyrs. This phrase merely suggests that God has a plan for the ultimate consummation of the age and that he will inevitably carry out that plan.

The breaking of the sixth seal symbolizes the release of God's judgment on the earth (6:12–16).

Chaotic destruction permeates the cosmic realm as the earth trembles, and the heavenly bodies change their form and fall from their places in the heavens. Nature becomes both the recipient and the cause of God's judgment. Terror reigns in the human realm as people from the highest levels of society to the lowest levels tremble at the thought of facing the righteous, sovereign God.

The Lamb

The lamb played a central role in the sacrifices of the Jewish people. The Jewish worshipers used a lamb for their sacrifice during the annual Passover celebration (Exodus 12:1–36), and in their daily sacrifices offered to the Lord (Leviticus 14:12–21). As early as Abraham's experience in the wilderness when God instructed him to sacrifice Isaac, the Bible makes reference to a lamb as an animal to sacrifice (Genesis 22:7). Consequently, when John the Baptist identified Jesus as "the Lamb of God, who takes away the sin of the world" (John 1:29), he presented Jesus as the new and final sacrifice by which God would atone for the sins of all people, for all time. In the New Testament epistles, Paul refers to the lamb as a sacrifice only once (1 Corinthians 5:7), and Peter includes only one reference (1 Peter 1:19). However, in Revelation, "the Lamb" again takes center stage. While John presents the Lamb as a sacrifice (Rev. 5:12), he also presents the Lamb as the one through whom God will manifest his wrath and ultimate judgment on humanity (6:16–17).

In verse 15, John probably listed seven different classes of people to affirm that God's judgment will include all human beings. No one will escape the sweep of God's judgment.

The Ultimate Result (6:16b–17)

John described God's judgment with the intriguing phrase "the wrath of the Lamb" (6:16). When biblical writers used the word *wrath* in reference to God or, in this passage, when referring to Jesus the Lamb, they were not implying hatred but rather the settled disposition of God's holiness to what one commentator calls "persistent and impenitent wickedness."[1] John explained the reason for the disorder and despair described in the sixth seal by referring to the manifestation of God's wrath. "For the great day of their wrath has come," he declared, "and who can stand?" (6:17). John echoed the warnings of the prophets in referring to a day so devastating that none among the wicked will be able to endure it (Joel 2:11, 31; Nahum 1:6; Malachi 3:2).

In John's culture, evil reigned supreme. The Romans, in all their oppressive power, ruled the world. John's vision presents an alternative picture of reality in which God's righteousness will prevail, not the world's wickedness. The victorious manifestation of God's righteousness will abolish the reign of evil. The exhibition of God's judgment will rescind Rome's oppressive power. Those who perpetrate evil on the earth will experience God's judgment. Those who remain faithful will experience God's redemption. Therefore, in this description of the horrendous manifestation of God's wrath against the wickedness of the world, John included words of hope for God's faithful people.

Implications and Actions

The world to which John addressed his vision is not that different from the one we live in today. Evil is found in every generation and culture. We see evil's power, manifested in global terrorism, growing with each passing year.

> ## Martyr
>
> A martyr is defined as "a person who is killed or who suffers greatly for a religion, cause, etc."[2] John described martyrs in Revelation 6 who were killed for their faithfulness to Christ and are awaiting the judgment of those who put them to death. Unfortunately, martyrdom for holding to Christian beliefs continues to occur around the world. For more information on this global crisis and to learn how to get involved in serving others, go to www.persecution.com.

Revelation 6 presents two basic messages in response to the evil all around us.

To God's faithful people, John's first message offers hope. This hope is not based on our circumstances, abilities, or intellect. It is hope found in God, who sits supreme on his throne, and in Jesus, the Lamb, who rules over the world as "the Lion of the tribe of Judah."

To the perpetrators of evil, John's second message is a clear warning that they will ultimately be brought down by the universal law of choices and consequences, as the righteous God orchestrates the end of time and metes out his judgment against evil.

Questions

1. What Old Testament book did John employ to describe God's judgment regarding horses and riders?

Lesson 4: *Six Seals Opened*

2. What are the parallels between the forces of evil at work in John's lifetime and the forces of evil at work today?

3. What are the implications of John's reminder to his contemporaries that they will have to wait for God to manifest his judgment against evildoers?

4. What is the basis for John's assurance that God will ultimately destroy evil?

5. Can you think of some ways in which our sinful actions as human beings affect the natural world around us?

Notes

1. Robert H Mounce, *The New International Commentary on the New Testament: The Book of Revelation*—Revised Edition (Grand Rapids: William B. Eerdmans Publishing Company, 1998), 153.
2. http://www.merriam-webster.com/dictionary/martyr (Accessed 2/15/16).

FOCAL TEXT
Revelation 7

BACKGROUND
Revelation 7

lesson 5

Intermission One: God's People Preserved

MAIN IDEA
In the midst of God's great judgments, his people will be preserved.

QUESTION TO EXPLORE
What is the source of our hope when all seems lost?

STUDY AIM
To explore the meaning of the images in this interlude and identify applications for my life

QUICK READ
God will ultimately identify, protect, and deliver those in every generation who have placed their faith in Christ.

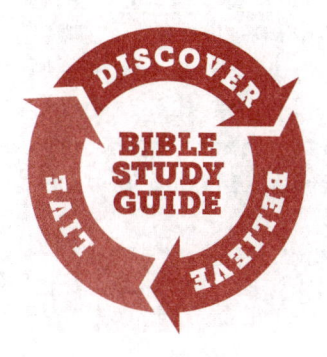

Introduction

When Michael Petroni adapted *The Book Thief*, written by Marcus Zusak, into a movie, he brought to the screen a fascinating story of family love and survival in difficult times. Set in a small German town during the Nazi era, *The Book Thief* tells the story of a German family and their illiterate foster child, Liesel. The father teaches Liesel how to read and instills in her a love for books. Some family crises take place in the greater context of the war, but bombing raids that send the entire neighborhood scurrying into underground shelters are a recurring threat. One night, however, the raid sirens fail to sound, and bombs obliterate the entire town. Liesel miraculously survives because she is in her reading room, the basement, protected from the destruction that engulfs everyone above ground.

The scene of Liesel's protection from destruction is a good visual for this lesson. At this point in the Book of Revelation, six of the seven seals have been broken, releasing messianic woes and bringing dissolution to the universe (Rev. 6:1–17). Before the seventh seal is opened, releasing the eschatological events associated with the end of time, Revelation 7 introduces an interlude, which explains what happens to believers when the forces of destruction are set loose on the earth. As the walls and depth of the basement protected Liesel from the destruction going on around her, God will protect his people during this time of worldwide catastrophe.

Revelation 7

1 After this I saw four angels standing at the four corners of the earth, holding back the four winds of the earth to prevent any wind from blowing on the land or on the sea or on any tree. **2** Then I saw another angel coming up from the east, having the seal of the living God. He called out in a loud voice to the four angels who had been given power to harm the land and the sea: **3** "Do not harm the land or the sea or the trees until we put a seal on the foreheads of the servants of our God." **4** Then I heard the number of those who were sealed: 144,000 from all the tribes of Israel.

5 From the tribe of Judah 12,000 were sealed,
from the tribe of Reuben 12,000,

from the tribe of Gad 12,000,
⁶ from the tribe of Asher 12,000,
from the tribe of Naphtali 12,000,
from the tribe of Manasseh 12,000,
⁷ from the tribe of Simeon 12,000,
from the tribe of Levi 12,000,
from the tribe of Issachar 12,000,
⁸ from the tribe of Zebulun 12,000,
from the tribe of Joseph 12,000,
from the tribe of Benjamin 12,000.

⁹ After this I looked and there before me was a great multitude that no one could count, from every nation, tribe, people and language, standing before the throne and in front of the Lamb. They were wearing white robes and were holding palm branches in their hands. ¹⁰ And they cried out in a loud voice:

> "Salvation belongs to our God,
> who sits on the throne,
> and to the Lamb."

¹¹ All the angels were standing around the throne and around the elders and the four living creatures. They fell down on their faces before the throne and worshiped God, ¹² saying:

> "Amen!
> Praise and glory
> and wisdom and thanks and honor
> and power and strength
> be to our God for ever and ever.
> Amen!"

¹³ Then one of the elders asked me, "These in white robes—who are they, and where did they come from?"

¹⁴ I answered, "Sir, you know."

¹⁵ And he said, "These are they who have come out of the great tribulation; they have washed their robes and made them white in the blood of the Lamb. Therefore,

> "they are before the throne of God
> and serve him day and night in his temple;
> and he who sits on the throne
> will spread his tent over them.

> **16** Never again will they hunger;
>   never again will they thirst.
>   The sun will not beat upon them,
>   nor any scorching heat.
> **17** For the Lamb at the center of the throne
>   will be their shepherd;
>   he will lead them to springs of living water.
>   And God will wipe away every tear from their eyes."

God's People Sealed (7:1–8)

Revelation 7 introduces this interlude by focusing on four angels poised to devastate the land and sea (7:1). At this point in John's vision, a fifth angel, more interested in intervention than in destruction, appeared (7:2–3). Two clues point to this angel's benevolent intent. First, he came "from the east." Ezekiel's help came from the east (Ezekiel 43:2), and the prophet Malachi looked to the east to see how "the sun of righteousness will rise with healing in its wings" (Malachi 4:2). So, an angel coming from the east signifies a good omen. Even more significant, we know this angel represents benevolence because it brought with it "the seal of the living God."

Apparently, the seal places a protective mark on the heads of those who belong to God. In this passage of Revelation, John used the Greek word *sphragis*, which was the same word used by the Apostle Paul to remind the Ephesian Christians that when they believed, they "were marked in him with a seal, the promised Holy Spirit" (Ephesians 1:13). We see a similar use of the seal in subsequent verses.

As with previous images, John borrowed from his knowledge of the past. Long before he described a mark on the forehead of the saints to protect them from destruction, Ezekiel used the same image (Ezek. 9). And long before Ezekiel described a divine messenger with stylus in hand who would put a mark on the forehead of the believers to spare them the divine wrath to follow, God instructed the Hebrew slaves to mark their doorframes with the blood of sacrificed lambs so the death angel would pass over their houses and spare their lives (Exodus 12:7–13).

John used the image of the seal to remind believers they belong to God and that God will protect them as they face the uncertainties of life, and the certainty of death. The seal also suggests that the work of redemption has been completed. No matter what happens, believers can rest assured in the hands of a God who will never let them go.

Who are the people to whom the fifth angel gives "a seal on the foreheads"? Some suggest these servants of God on the earth are the Jewish believers (7:1–8), and the multitudes in white robes are Gentile believers (7:9–17). More likely, the 144,000 are the believers on the earth during the time of difficulty, and the multitudes in white robes are the same group of believers in heaven, after the time of difficulty. In other words, the description in Revelation 7:1–8 covers a period before the trumpet judgments, and the description in Revelation 7:9–17 covers a period after the trumpet judgments, when believers experience the eternal blessedness God has prepared for them.

God's People Preserved (7:9–12)

Although the group identified in Revelation 7:1–8 is likely the same as the group identified in Revelation 7:9–17, in describing the latter group John emphasized size and diversity. They are "a great multitude that no one could count" and they are "from every nation, tribe, people and language" (7:9). Standing "before the throne" and "in front of the Lamb," they occupy a place of honor (7:9).

These people wear white robes (7:9). John mentioned white robes in only one other place, Revelation 6:11. There, God gave the white robes to those martyred with the opening of the fifth seal. These white robes symbolize purity, as they are made "white in the blood of the Lamb" (7:15). This reference to blood points to John's contemporaries, the other apostles, and to Jesus' death on the cross. It also refers to the shedding of the apostles' blood as faithful witnesses martyred for their unswerving faith.

In John's vision, the saints standing before the throne and in front of the Lamb also carried "palm branches" (7:9). Palm branches were used in the Jewish celebration of the Feast of Tabernacles to signify victory (Leviticus 23:40; Nehemiah 8:15). John probably used the palm branch image in this type of context. Instead of being defeated and annihilated by persecution, believers will emerge victoriously preserved. However, these martyred saints do not achieve their victory because of who they are, but because of who God is. They do not save themselves; the slain Lamb saves them. Recognizing again the amazing grace of God, they burst into a song of praise to the one who provides their salvation, that is, "God, who sits on the throne," and to the one in whose strength they have emerged victorious, that is, "the Lamb" (7:10).

John recognized another group that encircled the throne of God: "the angels" (7:11). John numbered them in the "thousands upon thousands, and ten thousand times ten thousand" (5:11). Why are these angels so ecstatic? Perhaps Jesus' statement in Luke 15:10 explains their response. Jesus told the disciples, "There is rejoicing in the presence of the angels of God over one sinner who repents." Imagine the joy of angels when they see standing before them a multitude of repentant sinners so large that it cannot even be counted! Their glorious doxology to God spontaneously flows from them as they face the spectacle of the redeemed (7:12).

God's People Identified (7:13–17)

Who are the people standing before the throne of God in John's vision (7:13)? The elder identified the multitude, first of all, as "they who have come out of the great tribulation" (7:15). Biblical writers often used the term *tribulation* to describe the inevitable suffering that accompanies following Jesus. Jesus used the term in this general way in John 16:33. Christians throughout the ages share this tribulation.

But the Bible also speaks of an intense time of tribulation that will come on the final generation of Christians, a tribulation that will be a climax to all previous persecutions (Daniel 12:1). John apparently referenced this final and climactic tribulation in the opening of the seventh seal. He assured his audience that those who are dressed in white robes have "come out of" the great tribulation. In other words, the tribulation does not defeat them, nor will it snatch them out of God's hand. Instead, they will prevail and will stand before the throne of God.

Lesson 5: *Intermission One: God's People Preserved*

> ### The Importance of a Seal
>
> The practice of sealing documents permeates the Old Testament. At times, the purpose of a seal was to guarantee the authenticity of a document. For example, Jezebel put King Ahab's seal on letters she wrote in her attempt to seize from Naboth his vineyard by seeking to convince those who received the letters that they came from the king (1 Kings 21:8). On other occasions, the purpose of a seal was to protect the contents of a document by preventing others from reading it before the proper time. For example, in Daniel's prophecy, God instructed the prophet to seal the document containing his prophecies concerning the future so that no one could read them until the end times (Daniel 12:4). John's description of the scroll and the seven seals employs both purposes. The seals on the scroll guarantee the message as words of God. The seals also prevent anyone from reading the contents of the scroll until the proper time.

John then added, "they have washed their robes and made them white in the blood of the Lamb" (7:15). These believers will not merely survive this period of tribulation; it will refine them into an incandescent faith so that when they stand in front of the throne of God they will be holy and acceptable to him, not because of their accomplishments for Christ, but because of his accomplishment on the cross for them.

John used the hinge word "therefore" to segue from the description of what the great multitude of redeemed people survive, to a description of what they will experience when they gather around the throne of God (7:15).

First of all, they will serve God. John announced that the multitude of believers serves God "day and night" (7:15a). John did not explain what kind of service they will do, but made it clear heaven will not be a place of idle indolence. Instead, believers will be productive in some way.

In addition, believers will be under the protection of God (7:15b–17). God will protect them by spreading his tent over them by providing for all their needs. Earthly desires will no longer plague them. Physical harm will no longer threaten them. Everything that brings pain to the human heart and psyche will vanish. There will no longer be any occasion for tears. Like the psalmist, they will be able to say, "The Lord is my shepherd, I shall not

> ## Every Nation, Tribe, People, and Language
>
> The diversity of the gathering before the Lamb of God (Jesus) and his throne will be amazing (Revelation 7:9). As you may have noticed, the nations have come to America. What is your church doing to reach the nations for Christ? One resource your church could use is the free Bible study materials provided in eight different languages by BaptistWay Press®. These resources are the result of the generous gifts of Texas Baptists to the Mary Hill Davis missions offering. You can access these studies at http://baptistwaypress.org/language-studies/.

be in want" (Psalm 23:1). For all eternity, they will experience the generous provisions of a loving shepherd and the consolation of a loving God.

Implications and Actions

John wanted his contemporaries to find security in the promises of God. We, too, can trust in these promises. First, we have the promise of God's protection, not protection *from* the difficulties of life but protection *in* the difficulties of life. Even the psalmist only promises God will lead us "through" the valley of the shadow of death, not around it (Psalm 23:4).

We also have the promise of God's provision, not of what we *want* but what we *need*. John's contemporaries needed food, water, and protection from the heat. Our needs today are different, but the unalterable promise of God's word is that his provisions are adequate.

In addition, we have the promise of God's presence, no longer *mediated* by someone else who has an inside track with God, but instead we enjoy his *immediate* presence. All of us, like the saints in John's vision, will eventually stand before the throne and in front of the Lamb.

Lesson 5: *Intermission One: God's People Preserved*

Questions

1. Can you remember a time in your life when God provided his protection in difficult times? Describe your experience.

2. What does it mean to say that God has completed the work of redemption in our lives?

3. What are the implications of John's statement that the number of the redeemed who gather before God in heaven will be "a great multitude that no one could count"?

4. What do the white robes worn by the redeemed signify?

5. What can we learn about worship from the song of praise voiced by the angels and the four living creatures who fell on their faces before the throne of God?

6. What did John mean by the redeemed will serve God day and night in heaven?

FOCAL TEXT
Revelation 8; 9:1–6, 13–15, 20–21

BACKGROUND
Revelation 8—9

lesson 6

Trumpets of Judgment

MAIN IDEA
God's judgment on his enemies will be comprehensive and unavoidable.

QUESTION TO EXPLORE
Does good really conquer evil?

STUDY AIM
To outline the events that accompany the six trumpets of God's judgment and identify implications for today

QUICK READ
Even as God metes out his judgment on sinful humanity, he still offers an opportunity for repentance.

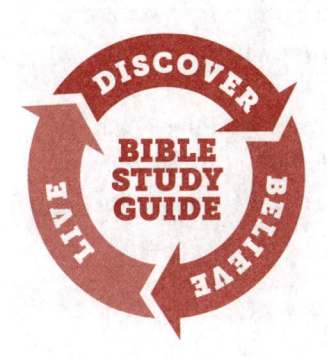

Introduction

Transport your mind to the first century and try to imagine the emotions of the early Christians. For years, Rome burdened them with persecution and restrictions; Christians were understandably miserable. In the midst of their despair, John assured them they could have hope. However, these words were meaningless unless something happened to Rome. As long as the people of God languished under Roman domination, they had no real hope. John therefore expanded his message of hope in Revelation 8–11 with the prediction that Rome would eventually fall. He describes the judgment of Rome within the framework of seven angels and their seven trumpets.

Revelation 8

1 When he opened the seventh seal, there was silence in heaven for about half an hour.

2 And I saw the seven angels who stand before God, and to them were given seven trumpets.

3 Another angel, who had a golden censer, came and stood at the altar. He was given much incense to offer, with the prayers of all the saints, on the golden altar before the throne. **4** The smoke of the incense, together with the prayers of the saints, went up before God from the angel's hand. **5** Then the angel took the censer, filled it with fire from the altar, and hurled it on the earth; and there came peals of thunder, rumblings, flashes of lightning and an earthquake.

6 Then the seven angels who had the seven trumpets prepared to sound them.

7 The first angel sounded his trumpet, and there came hail and fire mixed with blood, and it was hurled down upon the earth. A third of the earth was burned up, a third of the trees were burned up, and all the green grass was burned up.

8 The second angel sounded his trumpet, and something like a huge mountain, all ablaze, was thrown into the sea. A third of the sea turned into blood, **9** a third of the living creatures in the sea died, and a third of the ships were destroyed.

Lesson 6: *Trumpets of Judgment*

10 The third angel sounded his trumpet, and a great star, blazing like a torch, fell from the sky on a third of the rivers and on the springs of water— **11** the name of the star is Wormwood. A third of the waters turned bitter, and many people died from the waters that had become bitter.

12 The fourth angel sounded his trumpet, and a third of the sun was struck, a third of the moon, and a third of the stars, so that a third of them turned dark. A third of the day was without light, and also a third of the night.

13 As I watched, I heard an eagle that was flying in midair call out in a loud voice: "Woe! Woe! Woe to the inhabitants of the earth, because of the trumpet blasts about to be sounded by the other three angels!"

Revelation 9:1–6, 13–15, 20–21

1 The fifth angel sounded his trumpet, and I saw a star that had fallen from the sky to the earth. The star was given the key to the shaft of the Abyss. **2** When he opened the Abyss, smoke rose from it like the smoke from a gigantic furnace. The sun and sky were darkened by the smoke from the Abyss. **3** And out of the smoke locusts came down upon the earth and were given power like that of scorpions of the earth. **4** They were told not to harm the grass of the earth or any plant or tree, but only those people who did not have the seal of God on their foreheads. **5** They were not given power to kill them, but only to torture them for five months. And the agony they suffered was like that of the sting of a scorpion when it strikes a man. **6** During those days men will seek death, but will not find it; they will long to die, but death will elude them.

• • • • • • • • • • • • • • • • • • •

13 The sixth angel sounded his trumpet, and I heard a voice coming from the horns of the golden altar that is before God. **14** It said to the sixth angel who had the trumpet, "Release the four angels who are bound at the great river Euphrates." **15** And the four angels who had been kept ready for this very hour and day and month and year were released to kill a third of mankind.

> **20** The rest of mankind that were not killed by these plagues still did not repent of the work of their hands; they did not stop worshiping demons, and idols of gold, silver, bronze, stone and wood—idols that cannot see or hear or walk. **21** Nor did they repent of their murders, their magic arts, their sexual immorality or their thefts.

The Prelude (8:1–5)

Trumpets played a significant role in Hebrew life. The Israeli people employed trumpets while at war (1 Samuel 13:3) and while they worshiped (Numbers 10:10; Leviticus 23:24). In Exodus 19:16, the trumpet blast signaled the appearance of the holy God before his people. Eventually, the sounding of the trumpet would become associated with the judgment of God that will come at the end times. That appears to be the case in the text for this lesson. The trumpets announce the unfolding judgment of God.

The blasting of the seven trumpets that unleashes this judgment on the enemies of God flows out of the previous discussion concerning the breaking of the seven seals. When the Lamb opened the seventh seal, John explained, "there was silence in heaven for about half an hour" (8:1). "Half an hour" signifies a brief period. What was this short silence? Perhaps it was a silence of anticipation. John had described the instruments of judgment, the terror of the wicked during judgment, and the protection of God's people during judgment. In Revelation 8, all of heaven holds its breath to see what will come next. When God gives the seven angels the seven trumpets, everyone knows that the silence will soon be broken (8:2).

Following the silence, John described the smoke of incense created by another angel with a golden censer (8:3–5). The saints lifted their prayers to God, asking for deliverance, but apparently their prayers were insufficient. Only when the incense from the golden sensor engulfs the prayers did the prayers become effective. So, what is this incense? John did not explain, but we can conclude, based on his previous writings, that this incense represents the Savior's intercession in heaven for his persecuted church on earth.

Lesson 6: Trumpets of Judgment

The First Four Trumpets (8:6–12)

According to Edward Gibbon in *The Decline and Fall of the Roman Empire*, three primary forces led to Rome's downfall: natural calamities, internal corruption, and external invasion. John included these three elements with the sounding of the trumpets.

The destruction that comes after the sounding of the first four trumpets reflects natural calamities. The sounding of the first trumpet brings upon the earth a reign of hail and fire (8:7). At the sounding of the second trumpet, a huge mountain falls into the sea (8:8–9). When the third trumpet sounds, a blazing star falls from the sky and corrupts the water into which it falls (8:10–11). The sounding of the fourth trumpet causes the sun, the moon, and the stars to turn dark (8:12). The first four judgments announced by the first four trumpets affect nature in the four realms as classified in John's day: earth, sea, fresh water, and heavenly bodies.

Notice the recurring reference to "a third" of the various entities being destroyed. In each of the judgments following the sounding of the first four trumpets, John employed this term, which limits the destruction that will come at the sounding of these four trumpets, suggesting that judgment at this point is not universal but partial. God does not plan to annihilate the world at this stage but to call the world to repentance.

The Fifth and Sixth Trumpets (8:13; 9:1–6, 13–15, 20–21)

At this point in John's vision, an angel sounded a warning that the final three trumpets would usher in disasters that would make the first four pale in significance (8:13). This prophecy immediately becomes reality as the angel sounds the fifth trumpet and John saw "a star that had fallen from the sky to the earth" (9:1). Who is this star? Some scholars identify the star as an evil angel (Satan). Most view the star as another heavenly angel God sends to carry out his will.

God gives a key to "the Abyss" to this angel (9:1). The term *abyss* stems from imagery associated with the fathomless depths of the ocean (Genesis 1:2; Psalm 42:7). At some point, the term became an idiom for the

> ### The Abyss
>
> The word *abyss* is a transliteration of the Greek word *abussos*. King James translates the word as "the deep" (Luke 8:31) or "the bottomless pit" (Rev. 9:1). The Greek translation of the Old Testament (known as the Septuagint) uses this word to render the Hebrew word *tehom*, which describes the vast body of water upon which the earth rests, according to ancient cosmology (Genesis 1:2). By New Testament times, the word took on the more specific meaning of the abode of the dead or of evil spirits. For example, in Luke 8:31, the demons who possessed the Gerasene demoniac beg Jesus not to send them into the *Abyss*, for they do not want to go to the abode of the dead before their proper time. Romans 10:7 reflects this understanding by identifying the dark abode of the dead as "the Abyss." In Revelation, the word refers to a temporary abode of evil spirits, where Satan will abide for 1,000 years (Rev. 20:3). It is distinguished from the "lake of burning sulfur" into which Satan will finally be cast "forever and ever" (Rev. 20:10).

place of the dead and was also used to refer to a prison, which appears to be the meaning of "the Abyss" in Revelation 9:1. The Abyss is a closed prison which will imprison Satan for a thousand years (Rev. 20:1–3).

When the angel opened the Abyss, "smoke rose from it like the smoke from a gigantic furnace" (9:2). John's vision is that of thick smoke that obscures the light of day, obstructs breathing, contributes to illness, produces an unbearable stench, and besmirches everything on which it descends. It is as if hell itself breaks loose to pollute and defile God's creation.

Even worse than the smoke are the creatures that arise out of the smoke, locusts who "were given power like that of scorpions of the earth" (9:3). These locusts reenact not only Joel 1:2—2:11 but also the eighth Egyptian plague described in Exodus 10:1–20. Revelation 9:4–6 describes the devastating work of the locusts. Once more we see Christ's people spared the brunt of the end-time judgments. These locusts harm only those who do not have the seal of God on their foreheads (9:4).

These locusts will wield their destruction on people for five months (9:5). Some scholars identify five months as the lifespan of natural locusts. Others see the number five as symbolic. Since five is half of ten, a number that signifies completeness, five means this aspect of the judgment is incomplete, and there is more to come. Perhaps John used this term to indicate a short period of time.

The locusts have the power to inflict severe, but nonfatal pain. They will torment but not kill those they attack (9:5). John compared these locusts to scorpions of the earth. The sting in the scorpion's upturned tail releases a nonfatal poison that inflicts extreme pain. John used strong language to describe the plague inflicted by these locust demons with their scorpion-like stings, including torture and agony (9:5). The people attacked by these locusts with scorpion-like stings will long to die, but will not (9:6). Apparently the people will contemplate suicide but in some way, God will prevent them from carrying out that desire. They will instead remain alive to experience even worse agony in the days ahead.

John's description of the locusts in Revelation 9:7–10 reminds us that he did not use the word *locust* literally but symbolically. The locusts symbolize the demon hordes God uses as instruments of judgment. These creatures have the power and grace of horses (9:7). They wear crowns of gold (9:7). They appear with the intelligence of human faces (9:7). They show charm with feminine hair but ferocity with lion's teeth (9:8). They come with armored protection ready for battle (9:9). In the final part of the vision, John returned to the scorpion comparison (9:10). He repeated the purpose of the locusts swarm to torture the people and the limited nature of this judgment, which will last for five months.

Finally, John identified the "king" of the locusts and labeled him as "Abaddon" or "Apollyon" (9:11). The king of the locusts is either Satan or a demonic figure who represents the devil. The Hebrew word *Abaddon*, and the Greek word *Apollyon* are both translated as "the Destroyer." Satan, or an appointed underling, functions as king over the demons, and he is the exact opposite of the Lamb introduced in Revelation 5. The slain Lamb wants to save humanity; Satan wants to destroy it.

With the sounding of the sixth trumpet, we again see the four angels who held back the four winds of the earth (7:1), now release the winds of destruction (9:14). Instead of bringing about natural disasters, the destruction unleashed by these four angels will fall on human beings. Like the earlier judgments, this one is not universal. Only "a third of mankind" will be killed (9:15). God still provides sinful humanity the opportunity to repent.

> ## Wormwood
>
> The name of the star in Revelation 8:10–11 was "Wormwood." Wormwood is a bitter herb found in the Near East and is mentioned several times in the Old Testament (Jeremiah 9:15, 23:15; Lamentations 3:15; Amos 5:7).[1] It is always related to bitterness, poison, and death. In Revelation, this herb would embitter the fresh water of the earth, making it poisonous and resulting in chaos and death.[2] Of course, Wormwood is also one of the main characters in *The Screwtape Letters* by C. S. Lewis.

Between the sounding of the sixth trumpet and the seventh trumpet, John provided a progress report on the impact of the preceding six judgments (9:20–21). The limiting of the destruction of these judgments to one-third again indicates God's desire for those who have turned against him to repent. However, these whom God wants to save remain hardened against him, and continue in their idolatry (9:20) and immorality (9:21).

Implications and Actions

One theme arising out of this text is God's control of the future. Whatever happens in the future, whether it is the ultimate redemption of those who belong to the Lamb, or the judgment that comes to those who have rejected the Lamb, God is in charge.

The text for this lesson also reminds us of the malevolent purposes of the demonic powers in our world. Whenever demonic powers act (represented by the locusts in John's vision), they always want to do harm to those created in the image of God. But evil will not have the final word. Demonic forces are at work in our world, but ultimately God will have the final word. Darkness is not the final word in God's world; light is. Defeat is not the final word in God's world; victory is.

Lesson 6: *Trumpets of Judgment* 75

Questions

1. In the text for this lesson, who does the fallen star represent?

2. Why do we have trouble accepting the biblical message of God's ultimate judgment on sinful humanity?

3. Why are the locust and the scorpion appropriate models for God's judgment?

4. In what ways do we underestimate the power of evil at work in our world?

5. Can you remember a time in your life when God sent you a message that you needed to repent and return to him?

Notes

1. Alan F. Johnson, *Expositor's Bible Commentary*—Revised Edition 9, Revelation, Tremper Longman III and David E. Garland - General Editors (Grand Rapids: Zondervan), electronic edition.
2. http://www.gotquestions.org/wormwood.html (Accessed 2/18/16).

FOCAL TEXT
Revelation 10:1–9; 11:1–15

BACKGROUND
Revelation 10—11

lesson 7

Intermission Two: Faithful Witnesses

MAIN IDEA
God's servants will continue to witness, even in the midst of opposition.

QUESTION TO EXPLORE
How should Christ-followers respond as they face opposition because of their faith?

STUDY AIM
To identify current applications of the faithful witnessing described in this interlude

QUICK READ
Even when things are not going well around us, we need to faithfully serve Christ and courageously witness for him.

Introduction

Polycarp was a second-century Christian who served as the Bishop of Smyrna. In 155 A.D., the Roman authorities seized him. When he would not denounce his faith, they burned him at the stake. According to one tradition, one of the authorities said to Polycarp, "Renounce your Christ, or you will die" to which Polycarp responded, "Accept my Christ, and you will live." If that exchange accurately recalls Polycarp's final conversation, then he displayed the same kind of courage reflected by the two witnesses introduced in this lesson. Surrounded by multitudes who refused to accept their witness, and confronted by the beast who has emerged from the Abyss, the two witnesses continue to proclaim the truth about Christ.

This lesson explores the puzzling account of another scroll. It also showcases the two witnesses, their deaths at the hands of the beast from the Abyss, and their resurrections and ultimate ascensions into heaven.

Revelation 10:1–9

[1] Then I saw another mighty angel coming down from heaven. He was robed in a cloud, with a rainbow above his head; his face was like the sun, and his legs were like fiery pillars. [2] He was holding a little scroll, which lay open in his hand. He planted his right foot on the sea and his left foot on the land, [3] and he gave a loud shout like the roar of a lion. When he shouted, the voices of the seven thunders spoke. [4] And when the seven thunders spoke, I was about to write; but I heard a voice from heaven say, "Seal up what the seven thunders have said and do not write it down."

[5] Then the angel I had seen standing on the sea and on the land raised his right hand to heaven. [6] And he swore by him who lives for ever and ever, who created the heavens and all that is in them, the earth and all that is in it, and the sea and all that is in it, and said, "There will be no more delay! [7] But in the days when the seventh angel is about to sound his trumpet, the mystery of God will be accomplished, just as he announced to his servants the prophets."

Lesson 7: *Intermission Two: Faithful Witnesses*

⁸ Then the voice that I had heard from heaven spoke to me once more: "Go, take the scroll that lies open in the hand of the angel who is standing on the sea and on the land."
⁹ So I went to the angel and asked him to give me the little scroll. He said to me, "Take it and eat it. It will turn your stomach sour, but in your mouth it will be as sweet as honey."

Revelation 11:1–15

¹ I was given a reed like a measuring rod and was told, "Go and measure the temple of God and the altar, and count the worshipers there. ² But exclude the outer court; do not measure it, because it has been given to the Gentiles. They will trample on the holy city for 42 months. ³ And I will give power to my two witnesses, and they will prophesy for 1,260 days, clothed in sackcloth." ⁴ These are the two olive trees and the two lampstands that stand before the Lord of the earth. ⁵ If anyone tries to harm them, fire comes from their mouths and devours their enemies. This is how anyone who wants to harm them must die.⁶ These men have power to shut up the sky so that it will not rain during the time they are prophesying; and they have power to turn the waters into blood and to strike the earth with every kind of plague as often as they want.
⁷ Now when they have finished their testimony, the beast that comes up from the Abyss will attack them, and overpower and kill them. ⁸ Their bodies will lie in the street of the great city, which is figuratively called Sodom and Egypt, where also their Lord was crucified. ⁹ For three and a half days men from every people, tribe, language and nation will gaze on their bodies and refuse them burial. ¹⁰ The inhabitants of the earth will gloat over them and will celebrate by sending each other gifts, because these two prophets had tormented those who live on the earth.
¹¹ But after the three and a half days a breath of life from God entered them, and they stood on their feet, and terror struck those who saw them. ¹² Then they heard a loud voice from heaven saying to them, "Come up here." And they went up to heaven in a cloud, while their enemies looked on.

> **13** At that very hour there was a severe earthquake and a tenth of the city collapsed. Seven thousand people were killed in the earthquake, and the survivors were terrified and gave glory to the God of heaven.
> **14** The second woe has passed; the third woe is coming soon.
> **15** The seventh angel sounded his trumpet, and there were loud voices in heaven, which said:
>
>> "The kingdom of the world has become
>> the kingdom of our Lord and of his Christ,
>> and he will reign for ever and ever."

The Scroll (10:1–9)

In John's vision, we see another interlude before the seventh trumpet sounds. A "mighty angel" appeared, robed in a cloud, crowned with a rainbow, and covered with a light as brilliant as the sun (10:1). This huge angel was so immense in size it has one foot on the sea and one on the land. Perhaps John used this expansive imagery to indicate this angel's message of judgment will engulf the entire world (10:2). There is no mention of previously used limiting phrases such as "a third" (8:8) or "five months" (9:5). This judgment will be complete, and it will be final.

The angel had in his hand "a little scroll" which, unlike the earlier scroll covered with seven seals, "lay open" (10:2). The text does not reveal the exact contents of this scroll. Perhaps it clarified God's redemptive purpose, as it will be carried out through his church. If this is the case, God wanted John to understand this so he could communicate it to the church. Some scholars suggest the scroll contained the visions John revealed in the final part of the book of Revelation. We simply do not know. After John ate the scroll, he never mentioned it again.

The scroll's content prompted the angel to shout with a loud voice that evoked from heaven the "seven thunders" (10:3). Thunder usually represents the presence and power of God, and the number seven reflects perfection, so the text implies that in response to the prayers of God's people and the shout of the angel, God will respond with his full presence. Although the text does not specifically state this, many commentators conclude that each of

Lesson 7: *Intermission Two: Faithful Witnesses*

the thunders reveals an aspect of the response God will make to those who reject him and those who make up his people on the earth.

John proceeded to write down what he heard from these seven thunders, but a voice from heaven stopped him (10:4). What does this mean? Perhaps the voice forbade John from writing what he saw because the time had passed for warning the people of the world. Notice that the mighty angel announced there would be no more delay (10:5–6). The earlier judgments were to elicit repentance; these judgments would punish the wicked, "the mystery of God" would be accomplished (10:7). A *mystery* describes the work of God in relationship to humanity that cannot be known apart from the revelation of God. What God showed John through the revelation from the seven thunders, would now be accomplished.

Then a voice told John to take the scroll and eat it (10:8–9), which probably means he was to devour the book so he could thoroughly master its contents and incorporate them into his life. (The *eat* metaphor is also used in Jeremiah 15:16 and in Ezekiel 2:8.) When John incorporated the message of the scroll into his life, he felt both sweetness and bitterness (10:10). The sweetness came from receiving the word of God and understanding what

The Beast

The Old Testament uses the word *beast* to describe animals that are distinct from human beings (Ecclesiastes 3:18, NASB). The New Testament follows that same pattern (2 Peter 2:16). However, in both Old Testament and New Testament apocalyptic literature, the writers used the term to identify creatures that rise in opposition to God. Daniel alluded to four great beasts and explained that these beasts represent four great kings who will rise in opposition to God's kingdom (Daniel 7:2–14). John, in the Book of Revelation, recognized two beasts: one who rises out of the sea (13:1) and one who rises out of the earth (13:11). In the text for this lesson, John referred to a beast "that comes up from the Abyss," who will kill the two witnesses (11:7). Since the Abyss is identified with the waters under the earth, John apparently has in mind the beast who rises out of the sea. This seven-headed beast, who rises out of the earth, will eventually be judged by Christ (19:20).

God would do. The bitterness came in having to reveal the ultimate results of what God planned to do to the unrighteous, because God will carry out his judgment on his enemies.

The Measuring Rod (11:1–2)

The voice from heaven instructed John to take a measuring rod and survey the temple area (11:1). Again John channeled the Old Testament: Ezekiel had a vision of an angel with a measuring rod who measured the temple (Ezek. 40), and Zechariah had a vision of an angel measuring Jerusalem (Zech. 2:1–2). When we measure something, we identify the lines that separate it from its surroundings. Usually, the purpose of such measuring is to ensure these boundaries are honored and preserved. However, John measured only the inner court of the temple; the voice specifically ordered him not to measure the outer court "because it has been given to the Gentiles" (11:2).

John used symbolic language here, but to what do the symbols refer? Most commentators conclude that the temple represents the true people of God, the true Israel, and that the measuring of the temple implies that they will be protected from the destruction that is to come. Some suggest that the people in the outer court are those who claim to be Christians, but who are still a part of the world. In this case, the true church will be protected, but those pretending to be Christians will not be protected. Another approach suggests that the temple and the outer court both represent the true church and that the distinction John made is not between a protected group and an oppressed one. Instead, John distinguished between two different experiences for the true church. The people of God will experience oppression but the church itself, the inner core of the body of Christ, will be preserved.

The oppression the church will endure will last "for 42 months" (11:2), and the two witnesses God introduces will prophecy "for 1,260 days" (11:3), which is the equivalent of forty-two months. John used the time designations of forty-two months and 1,260 days as symbols for a limited period that will be marked by turmoil and difficulty. John assured his contemporaries that God would care for and protect them through it all.

Lesson 7: *Intermission Two: Faithful Witnesses*

The Two Witnesses (11:3–15)

Who are the "two witnesses" who "will prophesy for 1,260 days, clothed in sackcloth" (11:3)? Some commentators identify them as Elijah and Moses. These two witnesses do display similar powers to Elijah, who shut up the heavens with his prayers, and similar powers to Moses, who called down the plagues on Egypt (11:6). Other commentators translate the term "two witnesses" as *the church*. Those holding this view see the number "two" as symbolic, not literal, with the number two assuring that their witness is steadfast and dependable (Deuteronomy 9:15). Who gives this sure and dependable witness? It is the church. God will protect these two witnesses (the church) until they have finished their testimony (11:7).

At this point in Revelation, "the beast" will attack the two witnesses and kill them (11:7). John used compelling imagery in Revelation 11:8. He said the bodies of the two witnesses would lie on the street of "the great city," which is not Jerusalem but rather a symbol of what is ungodly. The text makes this clear by identifying the great city with "Sodom and Egypt." Sodom represents wickedness (Genesis 18–19), and Egypt represents bondage (Exodus 1). When John connected the crucifixion of Jesus with "the great city," he did not have in mind the location in which Jesus was crucified

A Faithful Witness?

Christ-followers are called to be disciple-makers (Matthew 28:18–20), which includes witnessing to others about the gospel. Consider the following questions related to this calling:

- How faithful is your witness?
- What is your greatest fear related to witnessing?
- How can ingesting God's word increase your confidence in sharing your faith?
- Who has God placed in your path who needs the gospel?
- Why is the need to share the gospel with others so urgent?
- What risk could you take to bring the gospel to another person this week?

(Jerusalem) but the evil that led to his crucifixion. In other words, Jesus was crucified by the same evil power that dominated Sodom and Egypt.

For three-and-a-half days, again meaning a brief period, the bodies of these two witnesses will be left on the street for everyone to see (Rev. 11:8–10). To a Jew, to allow a body to lie unburied symbolizes the utmost contempt and scorn. Viewing dead bodies left on the street symbolizes the attitude of the world toward the church. They will look at the church with scorn and disdain and gloat over the apparent demise of the church.

Although the world will trample the church during this period, God will not forsake the church, nor will he forget his promise to it. As Jesus was resurrected, so shall the church resurrect, as represented by these two witnesses (11:11–12). The suffering, defeat, and apparent extinction experienced by the church in the three-and-a-half days will give way to the church's resurrection, triumph, and ascension into the presence of God.

Meanwhile, back on earth, those who gloated over the demise of the church will experience the retribution of God. A tenth of the city will collapse as the result of an earthquake. Since a tithe belongs to the Lord, perhaps God exacts his due by killing a tenth of the oppressors. The earthquake will also take the lives of 7,000 people.

In Revelation, both the number seven and the number 1,000 have particular significance. Seven and ten both signify perfection or completeness. Combining seven with a multiple of ten suggests that the number of those who die will be the perfect number to fulfill God's purpose. The earthquake will not consume everyone, however. In John's vision, terrified by what they have seen, those who remain "gave glory to the God of heaven" (11:13). It is unclear whether this expression of faith is permanent or temporary. John reaffirms that God will protect his church. The church needs that word of comfort to face what unfolds in the remainder of the Book of Revelation.

Implications and Actions

The message of this text is a declaration for the church. We cannot know all the details of what the future holds, but we can know this: the future is in the hands of the one who was, is, and evermore shall be. When the collapse of the Roman Empire (and the collapse of evil) is final, God will be on his throne in full control, as he always has been.

This text is also a demand. Repeatedly, John placed a limitation on the extent of God's judgment. This partial judgment presents a warning to sinful humanity to repent, change their ways, and turn to him before it is too late.

Finally, this text demonstrates the sovereignty of God. God always reigns, even though it is not always apparent. At times, Satan appears to rule supreme in our world. Eventually, however, God will reveal the full royal splendor of his sovereignty. With all opposition abolished, it will be clear that the world is the province of God and his Christ.

Questions

1. Why does the mighty angel plant one foot on the sea and the other foot on land?

2. Why does the voice from heaven refuse John permission to write what he learned from the seven thunders?

3. As we devour God's word, in what ways is it as sweet as honey and in what ways does it sour our stomachs?

4. What does it mean when John says the two witnesses (the church) will die for three-and-a-half days?

5. What are we doing to prepare ourselves and those we care about for the eventual end of time?

FOCAL TEXT
Revelation 12:1–6,
13–17; 13:1–4, 11–18

BACKGROUND
Revelation 12–13

lesson 8

Saints vs. the Serpent

MAIN IDEA
As Christians face opposition from the powers of evil, we are to endure in faith, confident of God's victory.

QUESTION TO EXPLORE
What powers of evil confront God's work today?

STUDY AIM
To describe the actions of the powers of evil in these chapters and identify applications for John's day and ours

QUICK READ
God cast Satan, represented as a Red Dragon with seven heads and seven horns, out of heaven, which began a battle between good and evil that continues to this day.

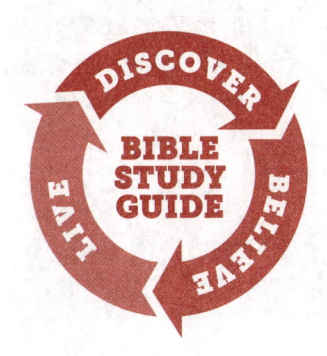

Introduction

Pastor Saeed Abedeni is an Iranian American pastor who spent three years in Iranian prisons. He was detained in Iran in the summer of 2012, and in 2013 he was sentenced to eight years for holding private religious gatherings in homes. His wife, along with others, worked hard to secure his release. During his incarceration, he was transferred to different prisons, each one notoriously more dangerous than the last. In spite of beatings, torture, and emotional abuse, he refused to denounce his faith in Jesus Christ. Pastor Saeed is just one of countless Christians tortured and even killed for their faith.

The Book of Revelation describes the source of evil and encourages Christians to endure and remain confident until the victory of Christ is completely realized. Jesus told his followers not to be surprised when the world hates them because it hated him as well.[1]

Revelation 12:1–6, 13–17

[1] A great sign appeared in heaven: a woman clothed with the sun, and the moon under her feet, and on her head a crown of twelve stars; [2] and she was with child; and she cried out, being in labor and in pain to give birth.

[3] Then another sign appeared in heaven: and behold, a great red dragon having seven heads and ten horns, and on his heads were seven diadems. [4] And his tail swept away a third of the stars of heaven and threw them to the earth. And the dragon stood before the woman who was about to give birth, so that when she gave birth he might devour her child.

[5] And she gave birth to a son, a male child, who is to rule all the nations with a rod of iron; and her child was caught up to God and to His throne. [6] Then the woman fled into the wilderness where she had a place prepared by God, so that there she would be nourished for one thousand two hundred and sixty days.

• • • • • • • • • • • • •

[13] And when the dragon saw that he was thrown down to the earth, he persecuted the woman who gave birth to the male child. [14] But the

Lesson 8: *Saints vs. the Serpent*

two wings of the great eagle were given to the woman, so that she could fly into the wilderness to her place, where she was nourished for a time and times and half a time, from the presence of the serpent. ⁱ⁵ And the serpent poured water like a river out of his mouth after the woman, so that he might cause her to be swept away with the flood. ¹⁶ But the earth helped the woman, and the earth opened its mouth and drank up the river which the dragon poured out of his mouth. ¹⁷ So the dragon was enraged with the woman, and went off to make war with the rest of her children, who keep the commandments of God and hold to the testimony of Jesus.

Revelation 13:1–4, 11–18

¹ And the dragon stood on the sand of the seashore.

Then I saw a beast coming up out of the sea, having ten horns and seven heads, and on his horns were ten diadems, and on his heads were blasphemous names. ² And the beast, which I saw was like a leopard, and his feet were like those of a bear, and his mouth like the mouth of a lion. And the dragon gave him his power and his throne and great authority. ³ I saw one of his heads as if it had been slain, and his fatal wound was healed. And the whole earth was amazed and followed after the beast; ⁴ they worshiped the dragon because he gave his authority to the beast; and they worshiped the beast, saying, "Who is like the beast, and who is able to wage war with him?"

• • • • • • • • • • • • • • • • • •

¹¹ Then I saw another beast coming up out of the earth; and he had two horns like a lamb and he spoke as a dragon. ¹² He exercises all the authority of the first beast in his presence. And he makes the earth and those who dwell in it to worship the first beast, whose fatal wound was healed. ¹³ He performs great signs, so that he even makes fire come down out of heaven to the earth in the presence of men. ¹⁴ And he deceives those who dwell on the earth because of the signs which it was given him to perform in the presence of the beast, telling those who dwell on the earth to make an image to the beast who had the wound of the sword and has come to life. ¹⁵ And it was given to him

> to give breath to the image of the beast, so that the image of the beast would even speak and cause as many as do not worship the image of the beast to be killed. **16** And he causes all, the small and the great, and the rich and the poor, and the free men and the slaves, to be given a mark on their right hand or on their forehead, **17** and he provides that no one will be able to buy or to sell, except the one who has the mark, either the name of the beast or the number of his name. **18** Here is wisdom. Let him who has understanding calculate the number of the beast, for the number is that of a man; and his number is six hundred and sixty-six.

The Dragon and the Child (12:1–6, 13–17)

To correctly interpret the Book of Revelation, it is important to understand the first-century context in which it was written. The Apostle John wrote the book to the seven churches in Asia Minor. One purpose of the book was to give encouragement to Christians facing persecution for their faith. God gave the Revelation of Jesus Christ to John during a time when Rome ruled the known world. There is debate as to who was ruling Rome during the time John wrote Revelation.

Possibilities include Nero, Vespasian, or Domitian. Domitian seems the most likely candidate because of his emphasis on emperor worship. He was only one of three emperors who received worship while alive; most emperors were worshipped after their death. Several cities requested permission to house temples dedicated to Domitian. All seven churches listed in Revelation existed in cities heavily influenced by emperor worship and the Roman imperial cult, a form of state religion in which an emperor, or a dynasty of emperors, were worshipped as demigods or deities.

Rome tolerated the Jews because they only worshipped one God; therefore, they were not required to worship the emperor. However, Jews who converted to Christianity were kicked out of the synagogue. Therefore, Rome did not extend the same tolerance to Christians. During the first part of the second century a new emperor named Trajan took power. He imprisoned and tortured Christians who would not bow down to Caesar. The churches

Lesson 8: *Saints vs. the Serpent*

mentioned in Revelation faced both persecution and the temptation to abandon the faith and worship the emperor.

Chapters 12 through 14 of the Book of Revelation appear between the trumpet and the bowl judgments. Although symbols and images fill the Book of Revelation, these chapters not only reinterpret traditional images, they also help translate other symbols in the book.

Chapters 12 and 13 introduce us to three important characters: Satan (the dragon), the false Christ, and the false prophet. The focus of this trinity is to oppose God and his people. John made it clear he was using symbols to relay his message. The first symbol used in Revelation 12:1–6 is that of a woman in childbirth. Many of the writers of the Old Testament referred to Israel as a woman in distress.

Although Revelation contains no explicit teachings about Mary the mother of Jesus, some scholars suggest the woman depicted in Revelation 12:1–6 represents both Israel and Mary. Other scholars suggest the passage contains reflections of Eve. The use of the sun, the moon, and twelve stars most likely points to the woman as a symbol of Israel, the redeemed people of God. The child is Jesus, who was born from the lineage of the redeemed people of God.

John used ancient myths to connect his readers with his description of Satan. Many ancient cults, such as those who worshiped Asclepius, the Greek god of medicine, used serpents in their worship and practices, and as symbols of their beliefs. John referred to the ancient serpent as *the dragon*, the same serpent that led Adam and Eve to disobey God. Jews often linked the serpent to the devil. John, like many apocalyptic writers, used the theme of a dragon to represent ancient myths and connect his message with readers. Jewish tradition and Scripture emphasize the dragon Leviathan, whom God would destroy. John described the dragon as having seven heads and ten horns, and on his heads were seven diadems. Later in Revelation the heads represent mountains, and the horns represent kings.

In ancient days, people often viewed stars as divine beings. In ancient Jewish culture, stars were believed to be angels. John used stars to relay the message that the angels who fell from heaven to earth were once righteous angels who renounced God. They amounted to one-third of all the angels in heaven. God punished them by throwing these angels and the dragon out of heaven. John was referring to the fall of Satan described in Isaiah 14:12–15.

> ## The Beast from the Sea
>
> John described the first of two beasts, the Antichrist, as coming out of the sea. This beast, like its master Satan, the dragon, has ten horns and seven heads. The ten crowns indicate it has more royal prestige than the dragon with only seven crowns. The blasphemous names written on the heads indicated false claims to divinity. Three animals were used to describe the monster, reminiscent of Daniel's vision in Daniel 7:1–6. However, John listed these animals in reverse order, thereby indicating a powerful political and military force. Rome was the powerful monster in John's day, and Rome received its power from Satan, the evil one. John described this beast as more powerful than Rome alone, but rather an empire of nations. The Antichrist will rise to power by counterfeit miracles (such as the healing of those fatally wounded), blasphemous words, and waging war against the people of God. He will divide the people on earth.

John reapplied this story by pointing out the ultimate goal of Satan was to stop Jesus from completing his mission. When Jesus ascended into heaven after his resurrection, he defeated Satan's plan.

Israel's history reveals that several times Satan attempted to prevent the life of the Messiah. Ezekiel referred to Pharaoh as *a dragon* in Ezekiel 29:3 (NRSV). In Jeremiah 51:34 (KJV), the prophet referred to Nebuchadnezzar as *a dragon*. Satan tried to kill Jesus shortly after his birth through King Herod's scheme, which was averted by the Magi. Satan thought he won when Judas agreed to hand Jesus over to be crucified.

In the Book of Revelation, John did not mention the death and resurrection of Jesus but highlighted his birth and ascension back to the Father in heaven. John did not attempt to teach systematic theology, but rather showed that God protected the child as he promised to do for all of his children. John symbolized God's protection again by revealing that God would care for the woman for 1,260 days.

John reinterpreted the myth of the baby being born as a god or emperor as indicating Jesus Christ. Jesus, the hero, was born through the redeemed people of Israel. John's use of a rod of iron indicates that Jesus is in view

Lesson 8: Saints vs. the Serpent

here. He is king, and he rules all nations. This story of Jesus links the history of Israel with its future and the future of the world. This section of the Book of Revelation is crucial because it holds the entire book together by revealing God's purpose in Jesus Christ.

Verse 13 repeats the events of verse 4. Because Satan could not defeat Michael and the angels, he is thrown to earth and sets his sights on the people of God, an easier target (12:7–12). The word *persecution* in Greek can also be interpreted *pursue*. Both meanings apply in the context of Satan. His hatred for the people of God led him to attempt to destroy them to prevent the return of the Messiah.

The Beast from the Sea (13:1–4, 11–18)

Several thoughts exist as to the identity of *the beast*. John borrowed many images from Daniel 7 but with slight alterations. Many Jews believed the fourth beast in Daniel represented Rome. Geographically Rome could come from the sea. However, John went beyond merely the idea of Rome to that of an evil empire. Beginning in verse 3 John used images that could indicate Nero as the beast, while also pointing to a greater theological conclusion.

This imagery would resonate with John's readers. Emperor Nero declared an official persecution against Christians. Jews also believed that Nero would one day return to power. Regardless of the actual person or empire, the beast is a symbol of the Antichrist. On earth, Satan will one day transfer his power and authority to the beast, and people will show their allegiance to him by worshipping him.

The contrast between the beast in this passage and the Lamb described in Revelation 5:6 is paramount. The question asked in Revelation 13:4, "Who is like the beast?" echoes the praise directed toward God in Exodus 15:11. The beast is the Antichrist, a fake Christ. Satan imitates Christ to receive the worship he desires. Ironically, by using a question originally directed at God, John answered the question, "Who is able to wage war against him?" The answer is Jesus.

John introduced a second beast in Revelation 13:11. This beast is the false prophet who has an appearance of the lamb but speaks as the voice of Satan. The true prophet leads people to worship God; the false prophet leads

> ### Worth the Fight?
>
> It is hard to imagine how Pastor Saeed Abedeni endured the suffering he experienced. His captors were trying to make an example of him to warn others not to share their faith in Christ. Through it all, Pastor Saeed did not renounce his faith in Jesus Christ. If you were in his shoes, would your belief in Christ's ultimate victory cause you to be passive or fight back against your captors? Why?

people to worship the beast. This beast is the greatest of all false prophets. The two horns without crowns indicate authority. The false prophet will institute economic measures to control people. In John's day, to withdraw from the established economic system led to starvation and even death. (In John's day, people were subject to an economic system connected to the worship of idols or meats sacrificed to idols.)

Today, blocking food sources to those who refuse to accept society's standards for buying and selling can result in starving to death, or, at least result in severe hunger. Revelation's "mark of the beast" (13:16–17) is figurative of the method that will be used by the governing bodies to keep track of those who worship the beast and those who do not. Everyone who wants to buy and sell will get a mark. A person will obtain the mark when that person worships and submits to the authority of the beast.

The number of the first beast is 666 (13:18). The number is used symbolically to represent the Antichrist. The number was significant to the readers of John's day, but today the meaning is not clear. Therefore, much speculation has been given to its interpretation. One possible interpretation is that God created man on day six. Six is the number of man. The number six is just short of the number seven which represents perfection. Listing the number of man three times could represent evil.

During this time, Jews and some early Christians used "Gematria" (an Assyro-Babylonian-Greek system of code and numerology later adopted into Jewish culture that assigns numerical value to a word or phrase in the belief that words or phrases with identical numerical values bear some relation to each other[2]) to interpret the meanings of words. Greek and Hebrew both

Lesson 8: *Saints vs. the Serpent*

used numbers as letters. Many commentators see a reference to Nero in the number 666. Also, when transliterated into Hebrew, the word *beast* comes out to 666. John's use of numbers reflects some of the Jewish apocalypticisms which his audiences would have understood. That is, the numbers 666 would alert the audience to watch for the attitudes and dynamics of anything and anyone who moved against Christ.

Implications and Actions

Satan moves around the earth like a roaring lion because he knows his time is short. John's warning to the seven churches in Revelation to be alert is an appropriate warning to God's church today. The battle we face is not one of flesh and blood, but rather spirit. Therefore, we cannot expect to fight with our strength and win. Christians must use God's word, the Holy Spirit, and prayer as spiritual weapons against Satan. The ultimate defeat of Satan at the hands of Christ should motivate Christians to fight on, regardless of how long the fight endures.

Questions:

1. How does knowing the future help you to live for Christ today?

2. Why does it feel as if Satan is winning today?

3. Why is the Book of Revelation so intriguing?

4. What evidence of this spiritual battle do you see today?

5. How do you prepare for spiritual warfare?

6. Describe the last spiritual battle you faced.

Notes

1. Unless otherwise indicated, all Scripture quotations in lessons 8–13 are from the New American Standard Bible (1995 edition).
2. https://www.google.com/webhp?sourceid=chrome-instant&ion=1&espv=2&ie=UTF-8#q=gematria (Accessed 2/18/16).

FOCAL TEXT
Revelation 14:1–13

BACKGROUND
Revelation 14

lesson 9

The Forces of Evil Receive Judgment

MAIN IDEA
God's followers can live in assurance that God will bring fierce judgment on all opposition.

QUESTION TO EXPLORE
Is following God worth it?

STUDY AIM
To consider the implications of this passage's teaching about God's judgment

QUICK READ
John encouraged his believing readers with the truth that although they faced fierce opposition, and even death, God would ultimately destroy all those who opposed them.

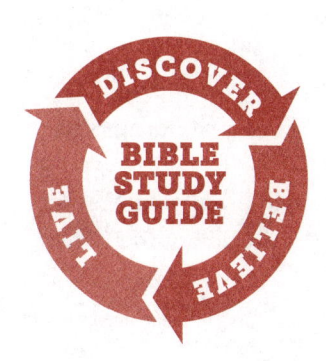

Introduction

Adolf Hitler killed himself by gunshot in Berlin on April 30, 1945. Saddam Hussein was executed in Iraq on December 30, 2006. Navy Seals shot and killed Osama Bin Laden in Pakistan on May 2, 2011. The stories of evil people who rose to power fill history books. They all shared the desire for world domination and all died without achieving this goal. Although more evil leaders will replace those who have failed and died, no power on earth will ever dominate the world. The earth and everything in it belongs to the Lord. He will ultimately overpower every foe and claim the victory for eternity.

> ## Revelation 14:1–13
>
> **1** Then I looked, and behold, the Lamb was standing on Mount Zion, and with Him one hundred and forty-four thousand, having His name and the name of His Father written on their foreheads. **2** And I heard a voice from heaven, like the sound of many waters and like the sound of loud thunder, and the voice which I heard was like the sound of harpists playing on their harps. **3** And they sang a new song before the throne and before the four living creatures and the elders; and no one could learn the song except the one hundred and forty-four thousand who had been purchased from the earth. **4** These are the ones who have not been defiled with women, for they have kept themselves chaste. These are the ones who follow the Lamb wherever He goes. These have been purchased from among men as first fruits to God and to the Lamb. **5** And no lie was found in their mouth; they are blameless.
>
> **6** And I saw another angel flying in midheaven, having an eternal gospel to preach to those who live on the earth, and to every nation and tribe and tongue and people; **7** and he said with a loud voice, "Fear God, and give Him glory, because the hour of His judgment has come; worship Him who made the heaven and the earth and sea and springs of waters."
>
> **8** And another angel, a second one, followed, saying, "Fallen, fallen is Babylon the great, she who has made all the nations drink of the wine of the passion of her immorality."

Lesson 9: *The Forces of Evil Receive Judgment*

> **9** Then another angel, a third one, followed them, saying with a loud voice, "If anyone worships the beast and his image, and receives a mark on his forehead or on his hand, **10** he also will drink of the wine of the wrath of God, which is mixed in full strength in the cup of His anger; and he will be tormented with fire and brimstone in the presence of the holy angels and in the presence of the Lamb. **11** And the smoke of their torment goes up forever and ever; they have no rest day and night, those who worship the beast and his image, and whoever receives the mark of his name." **12** Here is the perseverance of the saints who keep the commandments of God and their faith in Jesus.
>
> **13** And I heard a voice from heaven, saying, "Write, 'Blessed are the dead who die in the Lord from now on!'" "Yes," says the Spirit, "so that they may rest from their labors, for their deeds follow with them."

The 144,000 (14:1–5)

In Revelation 7, John introduced the image of 144,000 people who represent the twelve tribes of Israel, sealed and set apart. They will receive the mark of the name of the Father on their foreheads, which will signify the community of the redeemed. This seal will enable these saints to persevere throughout the final tribulation. These 144,000 appear in this lesson as an army with the Lamb, standing against those who will side with the beast and take the mark of the beast on their foreheads.

The place where these saints will one day stand is also significant. Mount Zion was God's dwelling place on earth. It was also a place of Israel's hope for salvation and triumph. According to Jewish apocalyptic literature, Mount Zion is also the place in heaven where God stands when preparing for war. The Book of Revelation depicts Mount Zion as the New Jerusalem promised for the future. Although Jerusalem lay in ruins after the destruction of the city in 70 A.D. by the Romans, at the time of John's writings, Jews continued to believe that God would one day restore Jerusalem's power and beauty. John's Jewish contemporaries looked forward to the day when Mount Zion would return the favor and destroy the evil empire.

In John's vision, the saints standing with the Lamb were singing. John also wrote about such singing in Revelation 5:9 and 15:2–3. In both instances, victory preceded the singing. In John's time, it was common to sing songs of celebration after a victory. In Revelation 14:3, the 144,000 sang a new song because they experienced the victory of the Lamb. John described their singing as the sound of many waters, the same description he gave for God's voice in Revelation 1:15. His description of loud thunder alluded to the voice of God, but also represented the multitude of singers too large to count, who were singing the new song.

In Revelation 14:3–4, John identified the 144,000 as chaste Jewish men, unmarried and undefiled virgins, devoted to God. (John likely used this symbolic metaphor because Israel's army consisted only of men. These men were instructed to stay away from women during times of war.) Symbolically speaking, in end times, these 144,000 men will refuse to commit immorality with the evil empire described as Babylon (14:8), whom Revelation describes as a prostitute.

The reward for following Christ on earth will be to follow him in heaven. John declared that these 144,000 blameless men will resolutely follow the Lamb. John then proceeded to describe the perfection of these men. God purchased them out of all humanity, not because of their good works, but to make them perfect (14:4b). John connected the Old Testament practice of first fruit offerings to God with his description of the 144,000, men who were viewed as a special offering to God. In Old Testament Jewish culture, the first fruit offerings involved only the best of the livestock or grains. John

Investment in the Future

John discussed the 144,000 saints who will receive the mark of the Lamb. They will stand with Jesus the Lamb on Mount Zion, the heavenly mountain of God, a place and position of victory. They will be victorious because they will overcome the authority of the beast through martyrdom. They will die for following Jesus rather than the beast. The imagery of the 144,000 confirms that believers experience victory over their oppressors, even in death. This reality encourages Christians as they invest in the future kingdom, rather than the present one.

used this symbolism to indicate the 144,000 will be united in their interests, and committed to following God.

In contrast to the Antichrist and the false prophet (who will speak lies to manipulate people in the end times), the 144,000 will tell the truth. Moral purity and truthfulness go together. These distinguishing marks of a Christian stand against non-believers who trade the truth for a lie. Followers of Christ should tell the truth regardless of the consequences.

The Angel with the Gospel (14:6–8)

In Revelation 14:6, John changed his focus from the redeemed to the unredeemed. He did this to contrast the future of believers with the future of those who choose not to believe. The first of three angels emphasized the judgment aspect of the gospel more than the grace of the gospel. The message of the gospel is grace to those who believe and condemnation to those who do not. The first angel's purpose was to preach the message of judgment to those still living on the earth. The angel proclaimed that all the earth bears witness to the glory of God. In contrast, the beast of end times prophecy will convince many that he is in charge of the world and the fate of people rests in his hands. The angel made it clear that wise people should fear God, not the beast.

A second angel announced the fall of Babylon. John used the word *fallen* twice for emphasis and to connect this description of Babylon to the fall of Babylon prophesied in Isaiah 21:9, and to highlight its future destruction. John also used the word *Babylon* to refer to the world system, which at the time of John was Rome. Jews were once captive to Babylon, but during John's lifetime, they were subjects of Rome. Both Babylon and Rome destroyed the temple. Both empires tempted Israelites to engage in idol worship and embrace their ungodly way of life. Jewish people who stayed faithful to God and did not engage in immoral idol worship or political corruption, suffered religious and economic persecution. Therefore, in Revelation, the term *Babylon the great* refers to all the wicked world systems.

In the last days, many people will believe the promises of a wicked world system to provide wealth, safety, and success to all who will follow. Once

> ### Maintaining an Eternal Perspective
>
> As Christians today, we face the temptation to compromise with the world and thus divide our loyalty to God. The commitment to be in the world but not of the world is a difficult one. Here are some helpful hints for maintaining an eternal perspective:
>
> 1. Read Revelation 14 in its entirety.
> 2. Verbally describe what happened to the people who followed the beast rather than the Lamb.
> 3. Conduct a spiritual self-check-up to see where you may have compromised with the world during the past week.
> 4. Connect with an accountability partner with whom you can share your desire not to compromise with the world. Talk with this person regularly for encouragement and correction when you stray.

they drink of the lies, they will become intoxicated and unable to discern the evil of that world order. They will give in to immorality and corruption. In contrast to the 144,000 virgins who will not give in to the seduction of Babylon, Revelation describes those who will succumb as prostitutes.

The Angel with the Message of Doom (14:9–13)

The third angel delivered a message to those who decide to follow the beast, warning that to choose the seemingly easy way means choosing a difficult, destructive path. A person who chooses to follow the beast (the world) elects to go away from God (13:9–10). John's word choice implies that, up until this point in time, there still will be an opportunity for individuals to choose to follow God rather than the beast.

However, those who follow the beast and receive his mark on their foreheads or hands will face the wrath of God. The wrath of God is far worse than any persecution the beast will pour out on the saints. John used the metaphor of *drinking from the cup* to suggest judgment. In ancient days, wine

Lesson 9: The Forces of Evil Receive Judgment

was often diluted with water. However, the full strength of God's anger will be unleashed on all who choose to cooperate with the wicked economic system of this future Babylon by drinking the wine of the beast. Although the wine offered by the beast will be strong, it will not compare the strength of the wine of God's wrath.

Those who chose the beast over God will face judgment that will result in extreme torment. The image of fire represents judgment; adding brimstone emphasizes the idea of extreme suffering (13:10–11). The fact that this torment will take place at the final judgment in the presence of angels reveals they will take part in handing down the punishment. Those who have denied the Lamb will be forced to acknowledge him, but it will be too late.

The smoke of torment is eternal, which signifies that those who follow the beast will suffer for eternity (14:11). Those who follow God will worship him day and night for eternity, and those who reject God will suffer for the same duration. Those martyred for the faith will enter into God's eternal rest, but those who have rejected him will never find rest. The angel's message is intended to encourage the saints to stay faithful in light of the alternative suffering awaiting those who do not follow God. The saints are warned to be patient, obey God's commands, and remain faithful to Jesus. Those who follow the Lamb will endure temporary suffering while those who follow the beast will suffer forever.

The angel also encouraged the saints with the promise of a reward for their faithfulness (14:12). Believers who persevere, even in the face of death, will be blessed with rest from their struggles.

In Revelation 14:13, a voice told John to write, which broke his time of meditation. John wrote a new blessing, reminiscent of the beatitudes of Jesus, to bring encouragement to those facing persecution and possible death. Although their faithfulness to God would result in persecution and possibly death, it would result in a reward that would last forever.

Implications and Actions

The temptation to follow the world's way rather than God's is always present. Many times it seems that those who disregard God and his instructions prosper, while those who remain faithful to him suffer or fail to move ahead. This feeling can occur when we gauge success by the world's standards. Hope for the Christian can come in the midst of battling anxiety and oppression by remembering that Christ has won the war. Every person who follows Christ shares in the victory that will one day be realized for eternity. It can be helpful to proclaim this truth out loud, along with other promises from God. It is good to hear the truth audibly, and because Satan cannot read our minds, it is helpful to verbally announce that he is defeated.

Questions:

1. What are specific ways you have suffered because you follow Jesus?

2. How does it encourage you to know God will reward your faithfulness?

Lesson 9: *The Forces of Evil Receive Judgment*

3. What would the beast represent in your life?

4. How would you explain the two sides of the gospel; grace and judgment? (See John 3:16–21).

5. In what ways do the 144,000 saints inspire you?

FOCAL TEXT
Revelation 15—16

BACKGROUND
Revelation 15—16

lesson 10

Songs of Victory and Scenes of Destruction

MAIN IDEA
God's suffering people can rejoice in the certain vindication of God's way.

QUESTION TO EXPLORE
Will God prevail?

STUDY AIM
To identify implications for the coming and certain vindication of God's way described in these seven plagues

QUICK READ
John wrote of seven angels unleashing seven plagues on those who take the mark of the beast. These plagues are reminiscent of the plagues Egypt suffered as God delivered his people.

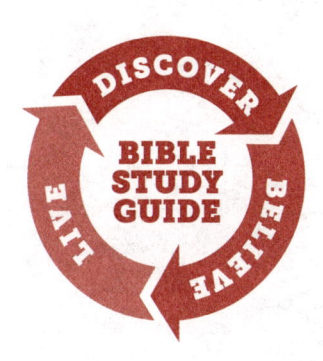

Introduction

As a Christian, what do you do with the problem of evil in the world? A member of a church I once served killed his wife, five-year-old daughter, and his father-in-law. This murder rocked our church. Amidst the sorrow and grief, there was anger, vengeance, and, for some, a desire to retaliate. As a pastor, I conducted the funeral for the family and tried to console the family of the murderer. I even had correspondence with the broken man who had killed his family. After a heart wrenching and graphic trial, a jury sentenced the man to die for his crimes.

It was interesting to talk with church members about how they felt about the man and the punishment he received. Christians who embraced Deuteronomy 32:35, where God said vengeance is his, admitted to a sense of peace and even strength knowing this man would answer to God. However, these same Christians were satisfied that the legal system punished this man for his crime.

Revelation 15

1 Then I saw another sign in heaven, great and marvelous, seven angels who had seven plagues, *which are* the last, because in them the wrath of God is finished.

2 And I saw something like a sea of glass mixed with fire, and those who had been victorious over the beast and his image and the number of his name, standing on the sea of glass, holding harps of God. **3** And they sang the song of Moses, the bond-servant of God, and the song of the Lamb, saying,

> "Great and marvelous are Your works,
> O Lord God, the Almighty;
> Righteous and true are Your ways,
> King of the nations!
> **4** "Who will not fear, O Lord, and glorify Your name?
> For You alone are holy;
> For all the nations will come and worship before You,
> For Your righteous acts have been revealed."

Lesson 10: *Songs of Victory and Scenes of Destruction*

⁵ After these things I looked, and the temple of the tabernacle of testimony in heaven was opened, ⁶ and the seven angels who had the seven plagues came out of the temple, clothed in linen, clean and bright, and girded around their chests with golden sashes. ⁷ Then one of the four living creatures gave to the seven angels seven golden bowls full of the wrath of God, who lives forever and ever. ⁸ And the temple was filled with smoke from the glory of God and from His power; and no one was able to enter the temple until the seven plagues of the seven angels were finished.

Revelation 16

¹ Then I heard a loud voice from the temple, saying to the seven angels, "Go and pour out on the earth the seven bowls of the wrath of God."

² So the first angel went and poured out his bowl on the earth; and it became a loathsome and malignant sore on the people who had the mark of the beast and who worshiped his image.

³ The second angel poured out his bowl into the sea, and it became blood like that of a dead man; and every living thing in the sea died.

⁴ Then the third *angel* poured out his bowl into the rivers and the springs of waters; and they became blood. ⁵ And I heard the angel of the waters saying, "Righteous are You, who are and who were, O Holy One, because You judged these things; ⁶ for they poured out the blood of saints and prophets, and You have given them blood to drink. They deserve it." ⁷ And I heard the altar saying, "Yes, O Lord God, the Almighty, true and righteous are Your judgments."

⁸ The fourth angel poured out his bowl upon the sun, and it was given to it to scorch men with fire. ⁹ Men were scorched with fierce heat; and they blasphemed the name of God who has the power over these plagues, and they did not repent so as to give Him glory.

¹⁰ Then the fifth angel poured out his bowl on the throne of the beast, and his kingdom became darkened; and they gnawed their tongues because of pain, ¹¹ and they blasphemed the God of heaven because of their pains and their sores; and they did not repent of their deeds.

12 The sixth angel poured out his bowl on the great river, the Euphrates; and its water was dried up, so that the way would be prepared for the kings from the east. **13** And I saw coming out of the mouth of the dragon and out of the mouth of the beast and out of the mouth of the false prophet, three unclean spirits like frogs; **14** for they are spirits of demons, performing signs, which go out to the kings of the whole world, to gather them together for the war of the great day of God, the Almighty. **15** ("Behold, I am coming like a thief. Blessed is the one who stays awake and keeps his clothes, so that he will not walk about naked and men will not see his shame.") **16** And they gathered them together to the place which in Hebrew is called Har-Magedon.

17 Then the seventh angel poured out his bowl upon the air, and a loud voice came out of the temple from the throne, saying, "It is done." **18** And there were flashes of lightning and sounds and peals of thunder; and there was a great earthquake, such as there had not been since man came to be upon the earth, so great an earthquake was it, and so mighty. **19** The great city was split into three parts, and the cities of the nations fell. Babylon the great was remembered before God, to give her the cup of the wine of His fierce wrath. **20** And every island fled away, and the mountains were not found. **21** And huge hailstones, about one hundred pounds each, came down from heaven upon men; and men blasphemed God because of the plague of the hail, because its plague was extremely severe.

Seven Plagues by Seven Angels (15:1–8)

John's Revelation letter was delivered to seven churches in Asia Minor. The purpose of the letter was to encourage Christians (then and now) during times of persecution and oppression. The seven angels and the seven plagues reveal that God will overcome evil in the end. Revelation 15 connects its readers to the plagues God used to deliver the Hebrews out of slavery in Egypt. The same God who delivered his people from Egypt is the same God who will deliver the Christians depicted in the Book of Revelation.

Lesson 10: *Songs of Victory and Scenes of Destruction*

John's vision of seven bowls reveals the judgments of God. John wrote about his visions in the order he experienced them; God did not necessarily reveal events to him in chronological order. John saw seven angels with seven bowls about to be poured out on the earth. This image symbolizes the final destruction of the Antichrist and his followers. In the last days, the seven angels will administer the full power of God's wrath on Babylon (the wicked world system), thus accomplishing God's goal: complete victory over evil.

In John's vision, there is a brief interlude of blessing before the angels pour out the bowls. He saw those who will be victorious over the beast and remain faithful to Jesus even in death. The word *victorious* is a synonym for *overcoming*. John saw those who will overcome the world system and refuse the mark of the beast. Earlier he described this group as God's army. Therefore, even though these individuals will not be able to buy or sell goods in the latter days, God will sustain this army. However, many will suffer and die for refusing to follow the beast.

The scene John recorded is reminiscent of the Israelites standing on the banks of the Red Sea after Moses led them out of Egypt and across the sea on dry land. Just as God destroyed the Egyptian army in the water, he is preparing to destroy the evil Babylon of end times. In John's vision, enduring saints sing the Song of the Lamb and the song of Moses (Exodus 15). Jews often sang the Song of Moses in synagogues during the first century. This song celebrated God's protection of his people from experiencing his wrath through the plagues. The Song of the Lamb celebrates the fact that Jesus, like Moses, saved God's people from his wrath. The saints depicted in Revelation will survive the tribulation and arrive on the other side victorious.

To highlight God's appropriate judgments, John linked the lyrics "Great and marvelous are your works" and "righteous and true are your ways." The Revelation saints will endure the persecution of the beast, yet consider God as right in his actions and attributes. In Revelation 15:4, John coupled the idea of fear with glory: "who will not fear, O Lord, and glorify your name?" This phrase points to the fact that all nations will one day worship the one true God, just as it reflects God's dominion over all nations. The conversion of all nations will occur at Christ's return. This image of all nations worshipping God is in direct opposition to the worship of the Antichrist, thus highlighting God's ultimate victory over Satan.

> ### The Importance of the Bowl Symbol
>
> In the Old Testament, bowls were used to pour out God's wrath on a rebellious Israel. In the Book of Revelation, bowls are filled with incense, which represented the prayers of the saints in 5:8. In chapter 15, bowls are filled with the plagues of God's wrath to be poured out on those who follow the beast. John described a bowl as an instrument used by the heavenly priests before the altar to vindicate the martyred 144,000. The bowls of God's wrath in Revelation 15 coincide with the prayers for retribution from the saints in chapter 5. The Jews were familiar with these bowls because the priests used these bowls, which were broad and shallow, as a part of their service before the altar in both the tabernacle and the temple. They may have been used to carry out the remains of the sacrifices.

The image of angels coming out of the temple in clean and bright garments symbolizes their work as holy. These heavenly angels respond to the prayers and petitions of the earthly priests and saints by pouring out the bowls of God's wrath. Smoke also fills the temple. (In John's time, worshipers and workers in the temple wore white to signify their righteousness. In the Old Testament, God's presence would fill the temple, indicated by smoke. At that point, no one was allowed to enter.) In John's vision, God's presence fills the temple as a response to the prayers of the saints, a symbol that God will vindicate the 144,000 by destroying their oppressors.

Bowls of Wrath (16:1–11)

In this part of his vision, John heard a loud voice from the temple, the very voice of God, proclaiming judgment from the heavenly temple for the followers of the beast who destroyed the earthly temple. In the final days, each of the seven angels will have a specific target on which to pour out God's judgment. The six bowls described here, as the trumpets mentioned earlier in Revelation, symbolize judgment on those who rebel against God.

The bowls mirror the plagues God poured out on the Egyptians at the time of Moses. The sores on those who follow the beast are reminiscent

Lesson 10: Songs of Victory and Scenes of Destruction

of the boils on the bodies of the Egyptians. The water that turns to blood symbolizes punishment of those on the earth who shed the blood of God's people. The heat of the sun increased to scorching temperatures and the lack of clean water symbolize drought. However, the Book of Revelation makes it clear that, just like Egypt's Pharaoh in the time of Moses, many people on earth during the end times will refuse to worship God, even though living conditions will be dismal because of God's judgment.

The plagues listed in Revelation and described as bowls of judgment reminded John's contemporaries of how God protected his people in Egypt, which produced confidence in them that God would again protect his people from his wrath. Likewise, these bowls give us confidence that God's protection for believers continues—for those believers living today and those who will experience life on earth during the final days.

The fifth angel's mission is unique because it is focused on the throne of the beast. It appears that under this judgment, the rest of the world will have light, and only the beast's throne of power will sit in utter darkness. In Old Testament times, the plague of darkness was a direct attack on the sun god of the Egyptians. This plague will humiliate Satan and dispel his powerful persona.

The Final Two Bowls (16:12–21)

This final series of God's judgments will complete his plan to destroy Babylon (Satan and evil) and usher in Jesus' return to earth. In Revelation 16:15, John repeated an earlier warning that Jesus will come "like a thief." Indeed, the great second coming of the Lord will catch many off guard. This statement points to the need for keen expectation of the day Jesus will return to earth—stay awake and clothed. In John's day, nakedness brought great shame to the Jewish people. John encouraged the followers of the Lamb to remain vigilant to the deceptive schemes of the devil, which would challenge their loyalty.[1] Nothing can stop the return of God; therefore, the people needed to be ready for his coming.

Bowls six and seven symbolize the final battle between good and evil, as well as the fulfillment of God's promises. In John's vision, the sixth angel dries up the Euphrates in preparation for the battle of Har-Magedon. At that

> ### God the Judge
>
> God loves and saves. God also judges. God's judgment is not a topic many people enjoy discussing, but it is part of his role. God judges those who oppress his people, but he also uses judgment to get people's attention so they will turn to him in confession and repentance. How would you explain God's judgment to a non-believer who is suffering and blames God?

time, the army of Satan will be released to gather for the great battle, along with the armies of all existing nations. The drying up of the Euphrates will allow the army of the kings of the East to cross over and invade the Holy Land. The battle will take place in Har-Magedon (Armageddon in other Bible translations), which is "the hill of Megiddo." The actual location and meaning remain a puzzle. Megiddo is in Northern Israel on a plain, and the valley of Megiddo was a place of significant battles. The name Megiddo means *place of troops* or *place of slaughter*. John may have seen it in direct contrast to Mt. Zion, where God would battle other nations.

The mention of frogs in Revelation 16:13–14 connects back to another Egyptian plague. John again mentioned the evil trinity, this time with frogs coming out of their mouths. The frogs point to the uncleanliness of the spirits. This image represents the speech and propaganda communicated by these evil spirits. Ancient people considered frogs unclean and vicious. They were also considered omens.

The seventh angel directs the final bowl toward the air. This action signifies God is Lord over the air, not Satan. God is sovereign over all things. He will judge Satan's entire empire. There will be no place for Satan to hide. Everything on the earth and in the air will be subject to God's reign. God will order the seven plagues to be unleashed by the angels, and after the seventh plague God will declare the judgment is over. Repeated in verse 17 of this passage of Scripture are the last words of Jesus before his death on the cross: "It is done" (finished). Again, John heard God's voice from the heavenly throne because God alone will determine the timing of the plagues. John also reiterated that God, the Lord Almighty, is in control of all things. He is the Alpha and the Omega, the beginning and the end.

Lesson 10: Songs of Victory and Scenes of Destruction

The lightning, thunder, and earthquake described in this passage of Scripture signify the revelation of God's glory. The primary focus is on Babylon, also known as the great city. God's glory will reveal Babylon's evil, and destroy it. This evil empire will experience the promise of the wrath of God, and will not stand. Its economic system, military might, and political influence will fall under the weight of God's power. Giant hailstones will fall just as they did in Egypt, killing many people. Those who survive this devastation will harden their hearts and refuse to repent. They will curse God and therefore continue to suffer and die in sin, unwilling to change.

All of the bowls filled with the wrath of God demonstrate that no nation can stand against the Lord God Almighty. This condemnation includes the old empires of Rome and Babylon and any empire that will ever exist. No human power can overpower God, who is above all. Not Satan, the Antichrist, nor all their armies can gain victory over God. He will accomplish his goals and fulfill his promises. Those who take the mark of the beast are doomed to experience the wrath of God. Those who take the mark of the Lamb, though they may suffer, will one day stand on the shores of the sea of glass, victorious. Their victory will lead to praise of the one who is worthy of praise. They will sing the song of Moses and the song of the Lamb, and his name will be lifted high. To God be the glory!

Implications and Actions

As Christians, we should live our lives expecting the return of Jesus at any moment. Awaiting his return provides hope and motivation to endure hardship, persecution, and even death for the cause of Christ. Our calling is not to make evil people pay for their actions, nor is it our job to administer eternal judgment. Remember, one day we will stand with the Lamb victorious. This reward should incite our praise of God. May our hope for the future compel us to obey and worship him. Although our enemies are many and powerful, no human power can defeat our God.

We must not merely focus on evil people or events that taint our world. We must focus our thoughts on the fact that Jesus promised us victory. One day, there will be no more crying or pain or death; the old order of things will pass away, and we will experience the new creation of our God.

Questions

1. How have you experienced the deliverance of God?

2. How does reading about the 144,000 singing beside the sea of glass encourage you to live for Jesus?

3. How do you explain the wrath of God in light of his grace?

4. What are some ways Christians can heed the warning in Revelation 16:15 and stay awake?

5. What is your response, knowing that even after the seven plagues, people will still refuse to repent?

Notes

1. Alan F. Johnson, *Expositor's Bible Commentary: Genesis*—Revised Edition 9, Tremper Longman III and David E. Garland - General Editors (Grand Rapids: Zondervan), electronic edition.

FOCAL TEXT
Revelation 17:1–6; 18:1–8

BACKGROUND
Revelation 17:1—19:5

lesson 11

Babylon Falls

MAIN IDEA
The improper use of wealth and power results in punishment rather than protection.

QUESTION TO EXPLORE
What dangers do wealth and power pose for us?

STUDY AIM
To describe the reasons for Babylon's destruction and identify implications for my life today

QUICK READ
God's judgment on Babylon warns Christians to stand against violence, oppression, and pride. We are not to become participants in Babylon's sins.

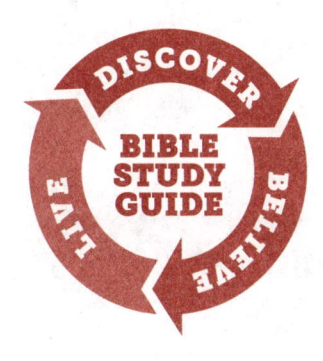

Introduction

I was in junior high when the Berlin Wall fell. I was old enough to recognize a pivotal moment in history but too young to grasp the event's far-reaching impact. The wall's destruction was a sign of things to come. A short time later, the Soviet Empire collapsed. The Cold War was over.

Americans reacted to the USSR's collapse with relief and vindication. The danger of nuclear war between the United States and the Soviets no longer loomed as a constant threat. We felt we had won the long Cold War; the "evil empire" was gone. What many had believed impossible was suddenly a reality.

For John's contemporaries, the fall of the Roman Empire must have seemed as unlikely as the fall of the USSR would have appeared to those living in the sixties and seventies. Rome was the nexus of civilization, power, and economic prosperity. It was also the center of violence, oppression, immorality, and persecution. Rome's misuse of wealth and power led to divine justice. The Book of Revelation pronounces judgment on Rome's oppression and warns Christians not to participate in Rome's sins. Our uses of wealth and power can look more like Rome than we want to admit. What dangers do wealth and power pose for Christians today, and what does it look like to use them well?

Revelation 17:1–6

1 Then one of the seven angels who had the seven bowls came and spoke with me, saying, "Come here, I will show you the judgment of the great harlot who sits on many waters, **2** with whom the kings of the earth committed acts of immorality, and those who dwell on the earth were made drunk with the wine of her immorality." **3** And he carried me away in the Spirit into a wilderness; and I saw a woman sitting on a scarlet beast, full of blasphemous names, having seven heads and ten horns. **4** The woman was clothed in purple and scarlet, and adorned with gold and precious stones and pearls, having in her hand a gold cup full of abominations and of the unclean things of her immorality, **5** and on her forehead a name *was* written, a mystery, "BABYLON THE

Lesson 11: *Babylon Falls*

GREAT, THE MOTHER OF HARLOTS AND OF THE ABOMINATIONS OF THE EARTH." **6** And I saw the woman drunk with the blood of the saints, and with the blood of the witnesses of Jesus. When I saw her, I wondered greatly.

Revelation 18:1–8

1 After these things I saw another angel coming down from heaven, having great authority, and the earth was illumined with his glory. **2** And he cried out with a mighty voice, saying, "Fallen, fallen is Babylon the great! She has become a dwelling place of demons and a prison of every unclean spirit, and a prison of every unclean and hateful bird. **3** For all the nations have drunk of the wine of the passion of her immorality, and the kings of the earth have committed *acts of immorality* with her, and the merchants of the earth have become rich by the wealth of her sensuality."

4 I heard another voice from heaven, saying, "Come out of her, my people, so that you will not participate in her sins and receive of her plagues; **5** for her sins have piled up as high as heaven, and God has remembered her iniquities. **6** Pay her back even as she has paid, and give back to her double according to her deeds; in the cup which she has mixed, mix twice as much for her. **7** To the degree that she glorified herself and lived sensuously, to the same degree give her torment and mourning; for she says in her heart, 'I SIT as A QUEEN AND I AM NOT A WIDOW, and will never see mourning.' **8** For this reason in one day her plagues will come, pestilence and mourning and famine, and she will be burned up with fire; for the Lord God who judges her is strong.

A Corrupt Empire (17:1–6)

At the end of Revelation 16, John described the destruction of Babylon, the evil empire, as a part of the seventh bowl of wrath. In Revelation 17, John began to describe Babylon's fall and the reasons for its destruction in much more detail.

The Book of Revelation personifies the church as the bride of Christ and Babylon as just the opposite—a prostitute. In his vision, John saw Babylon as a prostitute riding a scarlet, seven-headed beast. Together the woman and the beast symbolize the immorality, corruption, and violence of Rome, the evil "Babylon" of John's day.

In his vision, John saw Babylon as a "great harlot who sits on many waters" (17:1). The angel who showed John this vision later explained these waters represent "peoples and multitudes and nations and tongues" (17:15). The waters represent the nations and peoples over which the evil empire, visualized as a harlot, ruled. As a queen sits on a throne, the woman "sat upon" the waters of the nations. Both the kings and peoples of the earth participated in her immorality.

The interpreting angel carried John away in a Spirit-inspired vision to the wilderness, where he saw a woman riding on a scarlet beast. The woman John saw is the "great harlot" mentioned in Revelation 17:1. The beast she rides is a combination of the dragon and the "beast from the sea" described in Revelation 13. The beast is scarlet like the dragon, an image of Satan. The beast, often identified with corrupt leadership symbolized by Rome, demands worship and parodies the death and resurrection of Jesus.

The beast in John's vision has seven heads and ten horns. These horns represent seven kings; five who have fallen, one who is, and one who has not yet come but will remain a little while (17:10). The seven heads correspond to Rome's seven hills. Most Bible scholars also connect them to the Roman emperors, though it is difficult to identify which seven emperors correspond to the seven heads. Because seven is such a highly symbolic number in Revelation, it may be better to understand the seven heads as a symbolic representation of the emperors of Rome. The five who have fallen would refer to Rome's past emperors; "the one who is" would refer to the emperor who reigned over Rome at the time John wrote the Book of Revelation; and the one who would come describes a future emperor whose time was short. In other words, Rome's power would continue, but the empire's time was limited. Rome's dominion would come to an end.[1]

The ten horns are "ten kings who have not received a kingdom, but they receive authority as kings with the beast for one hour" (17:12). These horns probably represent either Rome's provincial governors or client kings. Both received their power from Rome and yielded to Rome's authority. John

Lesson 11: *Babylon Falls*

> **Ways to Apply this Lesson**
>
> Conspicuous consumption is one of the defining aspects of our culture. Practice simplicity by going on a spending fast. Limit yourself to only buying food and essentials for thirty days. As a family, discuss what you learn about your wants and needs.
>
> - Take a hard look at your entertainment choices. What messages are conveyed by the media you consume?
> - Think about positions in which you hold power or influence whether at work, church, or home. How do you treat those over whom you hold power? How can you use your power and influence to encourage and support those around you?

prophesied that these kings would join with Rome but eventually turn against the empire and destroy it from within (17:16–17).

The woman's clothing depicts ostentatious wealth. Scarlet and purple were expensive dyes to produce in the ancient world, and the woman is also dripping with gold, jewels, and precious stones. It is a picture of excess and greed. In her hand, she holds a cup filled with the wine of immorality and abominations. As those who worshipped the beast bore his name on their foreheads, the woman also has a name on hers: "Babylon the Great, the mother of harlots and of the abominations of the earth" (17:5).

In the Old Testament, Babylon was the pagan empire responsible for destroying Jerusalem and forcing the people of Israel into exile. John pictures Rome as a second Babylon because of its idolatry, immorality, and oppression of God's people. Rome was the source, or the *mother*, of idolatry and immorality because of the way Rome's influence exported these things throughout the empire. Rome's power and wealth encouraged people in its sphere of influence to worship the emperor and participate in Rome's idolatrous and immoral culture.

However, God judged Rome for more than the empire's immorality. John saved this decisive factor for last: the woman is "drunk with the blood of the saints, and with the blood of the witnesses of Jesus" (17:6). Being drunk with blood is a horrific image, particularly in the ancient world. Even pagans were revolted by cannibalism.[2] Rome's final and most serious crime was the persecution of God's people. Rome's oppression would not go unpunished.

Come Out, My People (18:1–5)

The rest of Revelation 17 describes the woman in detail and concludes with the beast's war against the Lamb. As a personification of Rome, the woman represents those who use their wealth and power to rebel against God and persecute his people.

Revelation 18 opens with an angelic pronouncement of judgment against Rome. The angel proclaimed that Babylon had fallen. Instead of a great and beautiful city, Babylon had become an empty and barren city where only demons and scavenger birds could dwell. John used the past tense to

Babylon, the Great Prostitute

The image of Babylon as a prostitute riding a great beast is one that may strike modern readers as offensive or anti-woman, but this is a place where we need to be careful about reading our modern sensibilities into the text. While it seems foreign to us, John's imagery of the woman Babylon draws on images his readers would have easily recognized.

The Old Testament frequently portrayed the nation of Israel as a woman, comparing God's love for Israel to that of a bridegroom for his bride. When Israel broke covenant with God and worshiped idols, the prophets depicted Israel as an adulterous wife or even a prostitute. The New Testament continues this imagery by describing the church as the bride of Christ.

Rome's idolatry and persecution placed Rome in direct opposition to the church. If the church was a faithful bride, portraying Rome as a drunken prostitute was a logical choice. John's imagery revealed the spiritual reality of Rome's corruption. Though we may not be comfortable with the description, we should not read it as supporting violence or as anti-woman rhetoric. We would choose different language today, but John's first-century readers would have understood his point: Rome's splendor was only a cover for its immorality, oppression, violence, and pride.

describe events that were still in the future. God's judgment was so sure that he could speak of it as if it had already happened.

God judged Rome because nations, peoples, and merchants had all participated in and profited from its oppression and immorality. Rome conquered others by its wealth as much as by its military might. Kings and nations swore allegiance to Rome in hopes of gaining a share of Rome's wealth. The Roman economic system also led to the development of a wealthy merchant class who profited from exporting goods to Rome while impoverishing those who produced those goods. Egypt, North Africa, and the Black Sea region sent approximately 400,000 tons of grain to Rome every year. This left the provincials in those areas to pay exorbitantly high prices for grain or to sometimes go without it.

Landowners often put so many resources into producing luxury goods for trade that they had to import necessities for their region, sharply raising the cost of living for the poor.[3] Some of these goods are listed in Revelation 18:12–13:

> . . . gold and silver and precious stones and pearls and fine linen and purple and silk and scarlet, and every kind of citron wood and every article of ivory and every article made from very costly wood and bronze and iron and marble, and cinnamon and spice and incense and perfume and frankincense and wine and olive oil and fine flour and wheat and cattle and sheep, and cargoes of horses and chariots and slaves and human lives.

Rome's obsession with luxury meant that it purchased wealth at the cost of human lives.

God called his people to come out of this system so they would not participate in Rome's sin and share her judgment. This separation was not intended as a call for actual physical relocation. Rome was a vast empire, and it would have been practically impossible to escape its influence. Rather, the summons to "come out" was a call to be in the world but not of it (John 17:14–16). Christians living in Rome faced a constant temptation to participate in Rome's oppression and idolatry.

Rome had no concept of the separation of church and state, irretrievably weaving commerce with idolatry. Temples served as banks and marketplaces. Joining a trade guild included honoring that guild's patron deity. Participating in the temple cults could help people accomplish financial transactions, show their loyalty to the empire, or provide the opportunity to become a Roman citizen.[4] Not participating in these cults made Christians vulnerable to social and economic pressures, as well as political persecution. However, participating in the empire's pursuit of idolatry and indulgence compromised Christians' loyalty to Christ. John urged his readers to stand firm in their faith and not participate in Rome's sin.

Judgment on Babylon's Pride (18:6–8)

God decreed that Rome would be paid back double for her crimes. As Rome had caused the nations to drink the wine of her immorality, now she would drink from the cup of God's judgment. In the Old Testament, thieves were ordered to pay back double for what they had stolen, not only restoring what they had taken but also making restitution for the theft. In the same way, God's judgment on Rome would be a double measure of her sin.[5]

Pride was the root of Rome's oppression and immorality. Revelation portrays Rome as a prostitute who believed she was a queen and would never face judgment. Pride, selfishness, and a belief that you are better than those around you lead to a host of sins. Though Rome believed she was above judgment, she could not escape the power of God. God not only judges oppression; he avenges it. Rome would fall before the might of God.

Implications and Actions

As Babylon, the woman on the beast represents Rome, but she also represents all empires and systems that set themselves up in opposition to God. Where we find people and systems that demand worship, indulge themselves in violence, and profit from oppression, we see the power of Babylon (evil) at work. Wealth and power can be used for good, but they also have an intoxicating force. When we seek to gain power and wealth and hold onto them at all costs, we become participants in Babylon's sins.

Lesson 11: *Babylon Falls*

As the people of God, we are called to stand against oppressive and exploitative systems. We do this in different ways. We can refuse to participate in the aspects of our culture that treat sensuality, violence, and exploitation as entertainment. We can use our pocketbooks to give preference to employers who treat producers fairly and pay a living wage. We can work for justice and speak for those who have no voice. Let us use our wealth and power to work for the kingdom of God, not in rebellion against it.

Questions

1. What are some ways in which our nation or culture is similar to the idolatry, immorality, and oppression of Rome?

2. How do you sometimes see people misuse their wealth and power? How can we avoid falling into that temptation?

3. In Revelation, God calls his people to "come out" from a system that profited from idolatry, violence, and exploitation. What does it look like for believers today to "come out" from similar systems?

4. Rome's temple system and emperor worship pressured believers to participate in idolatry so they could function in the economic marketplace. What are some ways that economic pressures today can pressure believers to compromise their faith? How can we resist that pressure?

5. One of the reasons Rome was judged is that Rome both profited from immorality and encouraged others to participate in it. What are some ways our culture encourages people to participate in immorality? How can we as Christ-followers be voices for truth while still speaking in love?

Notes

1. Mitchell G. Reddish, *Smyth & Helwys Bible Commentary: Revelation* (Macon: Smyth & Helwys, 2001), 329.
2. Craig S. Keener, *NIV Application Commentary: Revelation* (Grand Rapids: Zondervan, 2000), 404.
3. Ibid., 427–429.
4. Wes Howard-Brooks and Anthony Gwyther, *Unveiling Empire* (Maryknoll: Orbis Books, 1999), Kindle Edition, Chapter 3.
5. Grant R. Osborne, *Baker Exegetical Commentary on the New Testament: Revelation* (Grand Rapids: Baker, 2002), 641.

FOCAL TEXT
Revelation 19:11–21; 20:1–10

BACKGROUND
Revelation 19:6—20:15

lesson 12

The Return of the King

MAIN IDEA
Jesus will defeat Satan completely.

QUESTION TO EXPLORE
Where is history ultimately heading?

STUDY AIM
To describe the events in which Jesus will defeat Satan completely and to decide on how to apply their meaning

QUICK READ
One day, Jesus will return to defeat Satan completely. Our knowledge of Christ's victory should encourage us, as well as motivate our ethics and our evangelism.

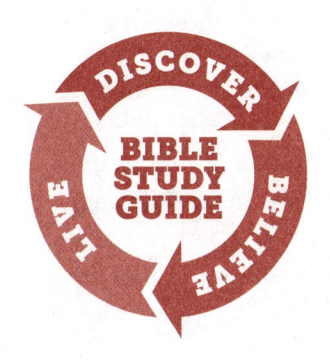

Introduction

You only have to catch the news to see the evil in our world. Girls are kidnapped from their schools, raped, and sold into slavery. Christians are beheaded in the Middle East and face persecution in many parts of the world. Gunmen walk into schools, theaters, and businesses and slaughter innocents. Some days, it feels as if evil is winning.

The good news is that Satan will not reign forever. We know the end of the story: Jesus wins! There will come a day when Jesus returns to defeat Satan and establish his victorious reign. Will we be ready to rejoice at his coming?

Revelation 19:11–21

11 And I saw heaven opened, and behold, a white horse, and He who sat on it is called Faithful and True, and in righteousness He judges and wages war. **12** His eyes are a flame of fire, and on His head are many diadems; and He has a name written on Him which no one knows except Himself. **13** He is clothed with a robe dipped in blood, and His name is called The Word of God. **14** And the armies which are in heaven, clothed in fine linen, white and clean, were following Him on white horses. **15** From His mouth comes a sharp sword, so that with it He may strike down the nations, and He will rule them with a rod of iron; and He treads the wine press of the fierce wrath of God, the Almighty. **16** And on His robe and on His thigh He has a name written, "KING OF KINGS, AND LORD OF LORDS."

17 Then I saw an angel standing in the sun, and he cried out with a loud voice, saying to all the birds which fly in midheaven, "Come, assemble for the great supper of God, **18** so that you may eat the flesh of kings and the flesh of commanders and the flesh of mighty men and the flesh of horses and of those who sit on them and the flesh of all men, both free men and slaves, and small and great."

19 And I saw the beast and the kings of the earth and their armies assembled to make war against Him who sat on the horse and against His army. **20** And the beast was seized, and with him the false prophet who performed the signs in his presence, by which he deceived those who had received the mark of the beast and those who worshiped his image; these two were thrown alive into the lake of fire which burns with brimstone. **21** And the rest were killed with the sword which came from the mouth of Him who sat on the horse, and all the birds were filled with their flesh.

Revelation 20:1–10

1 Then I saw an angel coming down from heaven, holding the key of the abyss and a great chain in his hand. **2** And he laid hold of the dragon, the serpent of old, who is the devil and Satan, and bound him for a thousand years; **3** and he threw him into the abyss, and shut it and sealed it over him, so that he would not deceive the nations any longer, until the thousand years were completed; after these things he must be released for a short time.

4 Then I saw thrones, and they sat on them, and judgment was given to them. And I saw the souls of those who had been beheaded because of their testimony of Jesus and because of the word of God, and those who had not worshiped the beast or his image, and had not received the mark on their forehead and on their hand; and they came to life and reigned with Christ for a thousand years. **5** The rest of the dead did not come to life until the thousand years were completed. This is the first resurrection. **6** Blessed and holy is the one who has a part in the first resurrection; over these the second death has no power, but they will be priests of God and of Christ and will reign with Him for a thousand years.

7 When the thousand years are completed, Satan will be released from his prison, **8** and will come out to deceive the nations which are in the four corners of the earth, Gog and Magog, to gather them together for the war; the number of them is like the sand of the seashore. **9** And they came up on the broad plain of the earth and surrounded the camp of the saints and the beloved city, and fire came down from heaven and devoured them. **10** And the devil who deceived them was thrown into the lake of fire and brimstone, where the beast and the false prophet are also; and they will be tormented day and night forever and ever.

The King is Coming (19:11–16)

Sometimes people talk as if the God of the Old Testament and Jesus are diametrically opposed. That is not an accurate picture. The Old Testament describes God's justice, but it also describes his faithful covenant love. The New Testament proclaims Jesus' mercy and grace, but it also proclaims his divine authority and right to judge. If we honor Jesus as the merciful Savior but forget he is also the coming king, we do not see him fully.

The Book of Revelation portrays Jesus as the warrior king. Its description of the marriage feast of the Lamb leads up to the dramatic appearance of King Jesus. He comes to issue judgment and declare Satan's final defeat.

In his vision, John saw Jesus as a rider on a white horse. In the Roman world, white horses were ridden by officials, rulers, and conquerors entering Rome.[1] Jesus came first as the Lamb, who sacrificed himself for the sins of the world. He will return as the conquering King of Kings.

John described Jesus by listing seven attributes. He is "Faithful and True" (19:11). We can trust that Jesus will keep his promises and return to put an end to Satan's evil reign because Jesus is faithful and true to his word. Faithfulness and truth are part of Christ's character, and he will not depart from them. John also said of Jesus, "in righteousness He judges and wages war" (19:11). Jesus judges and wages war in righteousness. He does not use his power for selfish gain or to get revenge on his enemies. In the last days, when Jesus rides forth to judge the earth, he will do so by holiness and righteousness.

John described the eyes of Jesus as "a flame of fire," probably describing both his holiness and piercing insight (19:12). He wears "many diadems." Unlike the beast who wore ten crowns, Jesus possesses his crowns rightfully. He wears many diadems because he is the king who is above all other kings. His authority is absolute and unchallenged. He also has a "name written on him which no one knows except Himself." Interpreters differ on what this phrase might mean, but one possibility finds it root in Roman cultic life. Magic practitioners in the Greco-roman world believed that knowing the true name of a deity or demon gave the magician power over that being.[2]

Christ has a name no one knows but himself. He is purely sovereign, and his power is beyond any human control. He wears a "robe dipped in blood" (19:13). Some Bible scholars believe this is a reference to Christ's sacrificial

Lesson 12: *The Return of the King*

> ## Ways to Apply this Lesson
>
> - The certainty of God's judgment should encourage evangelism. What are some ways you can naturally share Christ as you go about your day?
> - Think about how Christ has made a difference in your life. How can you share Christ by telling your story?
> - Memorize Scripture verses that point to our need for a Savior. John 3:16, Romans 3:23, Romans 6:23, and Romans 10:9–10 are good places to start.

blood; others believe it is a reference to the blood of his enemies. Finally, his name is called "The Word of God." As the Word of God, Christ is an agent of God's judgment on sin and evil. He will defeat the nations by declaring God's righteous judgment against them.[3]

In John's vision, the armies of heaven accompany Christ. Some think these are armies of angels, but like the saints, these armies are "clothed in fine linen, white and clean." (These accompanying armies probably represent the church riding forth with Christ as his victory escort.) Though described as armies, there is no suggestion that the saints engage in battle. In fact, there is no battle. Christ defeats his enemies simply by declaring judgment against them. Satan's power is no match for Christ's righteous authority.

The sword coming from Christ's mouth is a symbol of his authority and judgment. In John's time, the sword was a symbol of authority over life and death held only by the emperor and the governors. Here, it is a reminder that Christ alone has power over life and death (1:18).[4] He will rule the nations with a "rod of iron," destroying the enemies of the sheep. As grapes are crushed in a winepress, so the enemies of God will be crushed by the judgment of the Lord. Jesus has the right to do this because his authority and power are above all others. Christ conquered Satan through his death and resurrection, and at his return he will make that victory complete.

> ## Holy War
>
> Throughout history, the term *holy war* has sometimes been used to justify horrendous acts done in Christ's name. We should not use the warnings of God's future judgment to justify violence or *holy war.* The saints escort Christ to victory, but they do not participate in the battle. Revelation portrays Christ as the only one who has the right to judge—a right earned by his deity and through his defeat of sin and death on the cross.
>
> Although God alone owns vengeance, this does not mean we are silent in the war against evil. As citizens of a democracy, we have more options available to us than Christians living under the thumb of Rome. We can run for office and seek to change public policy. We can speak out for those who have no voice. We can support organizations that work for justice and oppose those who do evil. But we are to work for people's redemption, not their destruction. We work for justice, but God is the only judge.

Jesus Binds Satan (19:17–20:6)

John's next vision was of an angel calling the birds to come feast at the "great supper of God" (19:17). It is an ironic twist on the marriage supper of the Lamb. Satan will rally the beast and the kings of the earth to war against Jesus and the people of God, but the forces of evil will not triumph. Instead, scavenger birds will feast on their bodies after the battle. It is a grotesque image, particularly for people of John's time. Being left unburied was the ultimate humiliation in the ancient world—and this image recalls the fate of the two prophets who will testify against the beast in the last days (11:7–9).[5] The beast and his followers will receive the same judgment they mete out to others.

Although the beast will assemble a great army, Revelation does not depict a battle—only judgment. Christ's power is such that he does not have to go to war against his enemies to defeat them. His declaration of judgment is enough. The beast and his prophet will be bound and thrown into the lake of fire, and their armies defeated. This *lake of fire* is probably an extension of the idea of *Gehennah*. In the Old Testament, Gehenna

Lesson 12: *The Return of the King*

was known as the Valley of Hinnom. It was the place where some of the Israelite kings sacrificed their children to Molech. The name became synonymous with judgment. In Jesus' time on earth, Gehenna was the city dump outside Jerusalem. The fires in that valley never went out because of the constant burning of refuse.[6] Jesus himself used the image to describe hell. The beast and the prophet will perish in the fires of God's judgment.

Satan does not escape God's final judgment. John described how an angel will bind and imprison Satan with a great key, and then throws him into the abyss and "shut it and sealed it over him, so that he would not deceive the nations any longer" (20:3). This "abyss" is the prison house for demons. Satan is shackled, shut in, and sealed. There will be no chance of escape until the thousand years pass, but after that, he "must be released for a short time."

What are we to make of the "thousand years," also known as the millennium? Although this is the only direct reference in the Bible to the millennium, many disagree on how we should understand this thousand-year period in which the saints who reign with Christ are free from Satan's deceiving influence. There are three major views on the millennium: premillennial, postmillennial, and amillennial. Premillennialists believe that Christ will return to defeat Satan and then establish his thousand-year reign. Amillennialists believe that the thousand years is symbolic of this present age. According to the amillennial view, Satan's power was limited by Jesus death, but he will finally be defeated at the end of the church age when Christ returns. Postmillenialists believe that the church is to work to establish the thousand-year kingdom on earth before Christ returns. Most modern scholars hold either an amillennial or premillennial view.

Regardless of the timing, the millennium describes a period where Satan's power is checked, and believers reign with Christ in victory. In John's vision, after the great battle of Armageddon, he witnessed the first resurrection. He saw the souls of the martyrs who had been beheaded rise to reign with Christ. Is this first resurrection limited only to the martyrs, or are all believers included? The text can be read either way, but based on other references, it is likely the martyrs are a part used to represent the whole. All believers will share in the blessing of the first resurrection. They will serve as priests of God and Christ and reign with him during the thousand years.

Satan's Final Defeat (20:7–10)

According to Revelation, God will release Satan from his prison at the end of the millennium. He will once more go forth and deceive the nations and gather them for war. Satan's army will surround the New Jerusalem, but the fire of God's judgment will destroy Satan's forces. After this, God will throw Satan into the lake of fire. His defeat will be followed by the second resurrection and God's final judgment of humanity. At this final judgment before God's throne, all people will be raised and judged by their deeds. Death and Hades will be thrown into the lake of fire, and those whose names are not in the Book of Life will perish.

Why would God allow Satan to return and deceive the nations for a second time? Perhaps it is a reminder that time does not improve our sinful condition. During the millennium, the nations will know only Christ's merciful and glorious reign. Satan will have no power to tempt, deceive, or destroy. The peoples of the earth will only know Christ's goodness. However, Revelation describes that as soon as God releases Satan from the Abyss, nations will quickly reject God's truth for Satan's lies. The nations will rebel against God just as Adam and Eve did in the Garden of Eden. Time is not enough to change our sinful hearts. We need God's mercy and deserve his judgment. Only Christ can change us.

Implications and Actions

We are often more comfortable with God's mercy than his judgment. However, his justice is good news for us. Its means God will defeat Satan, and those who join with Satan in destruction and deceit will receive the judgment they deserve. Christ is our merciful savior. He is also our righteous judge and warrior king. We should honor him as both.

Our knowledge of God's judgment should spur both our ethics and our evangelism. If we will one day reign with Christ, we should live now as the holy people God has called us to be. We should also feel an urgency for evangelism. We do not know the day of Christ's return, but we do know those whose names are not written in the Book of Life will perish. Judgment is

Lesson 12: *The Return of the King*

certain for those apart from Christ, but God's offer of salvation is available to all.

Finally, this passage should propel each of us to ask, *Is my name written in the Book of Life? Have I trusted in Christ for my salvation, or am I still counting on my sincerity and good deeds to see me through?* God's mercy is real. So is God's judgment. You will meet Jesus at the cross, or you will meet him before his throne. Which will you choose?

Questions

1. When you think of Jesus, what ideas or pictures come to mind? How does the description of Jesus in Revelation 19 add to our understanding of who Jesus is?

2. Does it feel uncomfortable to talk about God's judgment? Why? How is God's judgment good news for us?

3. Why is it significant that Christ's accompanying army does not participate in the battle? Christ's proclamation of judgment is enough to defeat his enemies. What does that suggest about our response to sin and evil today?

4. How does it encourage you to know Satan will one day be finally and decisively defeated?

5. How do you know if your name is written in the Book of Life?

Notes

1. Craig Keener, *NIV Application Commentary: Revelation* (Grand Rapids: Zondervan, 2000), 453.
2. Mitchell G. Reddish, *Smyth & Helwys Bible Commentary: Revelation* (Macon: Smyth & Helwys, 2001), 367.
3. Ibid., 368.
4. Grant R. Osborne, *Baker Evangelical Commentary on the New Testament: Revelation*, (Grand Rapids: Baker, 2002), 684–685.
5. Ibid., 690.
6. Ibid.

FOCAL TEXT
Revelation 21:1–8;
22:1–7, 16–17

BACKGROUND
Revelation 21—22

lesson 13

A New Heaven and a New Earth

MAIN IDEA
God will make all things new and good for those who place their faith in Jesus.

QUESTION TO EXPLORE
How can everything be made good again?

STUDY AIM
To embrace the hope found in Revelation's description of a new heaven and new earth

QUICK READ
Jesus' victory ensures the wonders and blessings of life in the presence of God for those who place their faith in Jesus. Christ's victory is our source of hope.

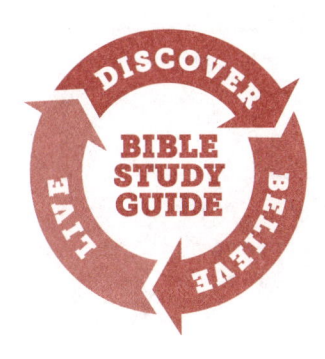

Introduction

Our first home was a fixer-upper: dark, dated paneling, damaged flooring, odd paint colors, and disintegrating kitchen cabinets. It needed work. But with time and help from some loving friends, we got it into shape. It was small, but it was ours, and it was a good first home for our growing family.

God's creation of a new heaven and earth is going to be more than just a renovation; it will be a transformation. God will make a new home where he will dwell in the midst of his people, and we will enjoy God's presence forever. No more sin. No more death. No sorrow, tears, or mourning. All the pain and heartaches of our broken world will be washed away in the joy of Christ's presence with us forever. We will live the good life God intended from the beginning.

Revelation 21:1–8

1 Then I saw a new heaven and a new earth; for the first heaven and the first earth passed away, and there is no longer any sea. **2** And I saw the holy city, new Jerusalem, coming down out of heaven from God, made ready as a bride adorned for her husband. **3** And I heard a loud voice from the throne, saying, "Behold, the tabernacle of God is among men, and He will dwell among them, and they shall be His people, and God Himself will be among them, **4** and He will wipe away every tear from their eyes; and there will no longer be any death; there will no longer be any mourning, or crying, or pain; the first things have passed away."

5 And He who sits on the throne said, "Behold, I am making all things new." And He said, "Write, for these words are faithful and true." **6** Then He said to me, "It is done. I am the Alpha and the Omega, the beginning and the end. I will give to the one who thirsts from the spring of the water of life without cost. **7** He who overcomes will inherit these things, and I will be his God and he will be My son. **8** But for the cowardly and unbelieving and abominable and murderers and immoral persons and sorcerers and idolaters and all liars, their part will be in the lake that burns with fire and brimstone, which is the second death.

Lesson 13: *A New Heaven and a New Earth*

Revelation 22:1–7, 16–17

1 Then he showed me a river of the water of life, clear as crystal, coming from the throne of God and of the Lamb, **2** in the middle of its street. On either side of the river was the tree of life, bearing twelve kinds *of* fruit, yielding its fruit every month; and the leaves of the tree were for the healing of the nations. **3** There will no longer be any curse; and the throne of God and of the Lamb will be in it, and His bond-servants will serve Him; **4** they will see His face, and His name will be on their foreheads. **5** And there will no longer be any night; and they will not have need of the light of a lamp nor the light of the sun, because the Lord God will illumine them; and they will reign forever and ever.

6 And he said to me, "These words are faithful and true"; and the Lord, the God of the spirits of the prophets, sent His angel to show to His bond-servants the things which must soon take place.

7 "And behold, I am coming quickly. Blessed is he who heeds the words of the prophecy of this book."

• • • • • • • • • • • • • • • • • •

16 "I, Jesus, have sent My angel to testify to you these things for the churches. I am the root and the descendant of David, the bright morning star."

17 The Spirit and the bride say, "Come." And let the one who hears say, "Come." And let the one who is thirsty come; let the one who wishes take the water of life without cost.

All Things New (21:1–8)

John's vision of the final judgment preceded a glimpse into the glorious future that awaits the people of God. The apostle saw a new heaven and a new earth, for "the first heaven and the first earth had passed away."

Paul wrote that creation groans for the day of redemption (Romans 8:22). Sin doesn't just affect us; it affects creation itself. The world as we know it is tainted and twisted by the power of sin. As we will enjoy heaven in glorified and resurrected bodies, so will the created order be transformed, redeemed, and made new by God's great mercy. The new heaven and new earth are the home God will create to enjoy with his people.

As a part of this new earth, John saw "the holy city, new Jerusalem, coming down out of heaven from God, made ready as a bride adorned for her husband" (Rev. 21:2). As described later in the chapter, the New Jerusalem is massive—approximately 1,500 miles on all sides—and made from gold and precious jewels. Whereas Babylon describes both a place and the people who rebel against God, the New Jerusalem represents both the place where God's people will dwell and the people themselves.[1]

Interestingly, the New Jerusalem is described as being a cube—the same shape of the Holy of Holies, the place within the tabernacle where God's presence dwelled. In his vision, John heard a loud voice announce that "the tabernacle of God is among men, and He will dwell among them, and they shall be his people and God Himself will be among them" (21:3). There will be no temple or tabernacle in the new creation because God himself will dwell among us. We will live in the midst of the Holy of Holies, forever living in the presence of the Lord. There will be no more need for a priest or intermediary; no need for a veil to separate us from God's presence. We will see the Lord face-to-face, enjoying all the intimacy and blessing of God's presence.

As part of that blessing, God will remove all causes of mourning and sorrow. Sin and death will cease to exist; we will have no more cause for weeping. What a powerful promise for the churches who first read the Book of Revelation! Though they lived in times of poverty and persecution, they found comfort in knowing it would one day come to an end. The same truth can encourage us. Cancer, depression, miscarriage, debt, hunger, grief—all the trials and turmoil of our sin-stained world will be swept away in God's presence.

In John's vision, God himself promised that he is making all things new and commanded John to record these truths, for "these words are true and faithful" (21:5). This communication is only the second time God directly speaks in the Book of Revelation. In a sense, God used his own character as collateral to prove that his promises are trustworthy.[2] If we cannot trust the words of the one who is truth, whom can we trust? God is faithful, and we can trust him to keep his promises.

In the final pages of the Book of Revelation, God declares, "It is done" (21:6). Though the new heaven and new earth lie in the future from our point of view, God's promise makes them so certain he can speak of it as already accomplished. Our God, the Alpha and the Omega, the one who began all history and who will bring it to completion, has declared that it will be so. Nothing will thwart his purposes. The one who thirsts for God's presence will drink from the life-giving water of the Spirit. Those who overcome—who remain faithful to Christ despite opposition—will inherit all God's promises and dwell with God in intimacy forever.

And yet there remains a warning for those who do not overcome. Revelation 21:8 contains a vice list similar to others found in the New Testament, but the vices (sins) listed in this verse are connected to others described in Revelation. The "cowardly" are those who do not overcome or remain faithful. Unbelievers are those who refused to trust in Christ; "abominations" often refers to idolatry and may describe those who participate in emperor worship or other pagan cults. "Murderers" probably describes those who have killed and martyred God's people. "Immoral persons" could

---

Esther Ahn Kim: An Overcomer

During the 1930s, Japan began an intense cultural assimilation campaign in Japan-occupied Korea. Japan forced Koreans to adopt Japanese names and forbade them to speak Korean. Japan also required Koreans to participate in ceremonies at Shinto shrines. Those who refused faced harsh retribution.

In 1939, the school at which Ahn Ei Sook taught was required to attend a gathering at a regional shrine. Ei Sook remembered Shadrach, Meshach, and Abednego. When everyone else bowed, she remained standing and stared at the sky.

As punishment, Ei Sook endured six years of harsh imprisonment, but she continued to be faithful. She gave a Bible to one of her Japanese guards and demonstrated kindness to her fellow prisoners. She proclaimed Christ even during her trial. Only fourteen of the thirty-four Christians who entered Pyongyang prison in 1940 survived.

After the war, Ei Sook and her husband immigrated to the United States and adopted the names of Don and Esther Ahn Kim. Don went on to found the second Southern Baptist Korean congregation in the United States.[5]

refer either to sexual immorality or idolatry, and sorcerers and idolaters also describe those who practice magic or who participate in the pagan cults. "Liars" are either false prophets or those who lie about their faithfulness to Christ.[3] None of these will enter the New Jerusalem; instead they will face the fires of God's judgment. Only those who are faithful to Christ's lordship will enjoy God's presence in eternity.

The River and the Tree (22:1–7)

A river of the "water of life" is at the center of John's vision of paradise. The river flows from the throne of God through the middle of the main street of the New Jerusalem. Jesus compared the Holy Spirit to living water (John 4:14; 7:38). In eternity, God's people will have free access to the life-giving water of the Spirit.

John's description of the tree of life growing on either side of the river probably means rows of trees flanking the river on either side. Where Eden only had one tree of life, the New Jerusalem will have a grove.[4] What humanity lost access to in Eden will be regained in eternity. We will no longer be barred from eating from the tree of life; rather we will be invited to feast upon its fruit.

There is no curse for those who dwell in God's presence. Since Eden, life in this world has been marred by the curse of sin and death. In the new

Applying this Lesson

- Think about situations in which you feel pressured to compromise your faith. What might it look like to be an overcomer in your circumstances?
- What groups in your community minister to those who need to hear the hope in this passage? How can you assist them?
- Think of someone who is facing the first holiday, anniversary, or birthday without a loved one. Pray for that person and write him or her an encouraging note incorporating the truths of this lesson.

Lesson 13: A New Heaven and a New Earth

creation, sin's curse will be washed away. Those who have followed Christ will spend eternity in his presence, and we will see God face-to-face. Moses only saw God's back (Exodus 33:23), but we will experience the joy of being in God's presence with no barriers of time, space, or sin between us. What Moses longed for we will get to see. God's name will be on our foreheads, marking us permanently as his own.

There will be no night in the New Jerusalem, nor any need for the sun. Both the physical darkness of night and the symbolic darkness of sin will be gone. God's glory will be all the light we need. God also promises we will reign with him forever. Though in this world, suffering, persecution, and rejection mar our lives, this is not the end of our stories. God has ordained that in eternity the people of God will reign with Christ and share in his victory.

We can trust these things will be so because we serve a God who keeps his promises. Christ promises he is coming soon, and we should take him at his word. We do not know the day or the hour of Christ's return, but we know his return is certain, and every day brings us closer than the last. We are to live in expectancy, both anticipating and preparing for the day Christ returns. If we heed the words of Revelation, resist compromise, and remain faithful, we will receive the blessings Christ has in store for his people.

The Invitation to Come (22:16–17)

We can trust that the words of the Book of Revelation are true because Jesus said they would be so. As God did in Revelation 21:5, Jesus essentially swears by himself in Revelation 22:16–17, using his character to prove he will keep his promises. Jesus is the "root and descendant of David." God promised that the Messiah would come from David's line, and as a descendant of David, Jesus is the fulfillment of that promise. But Jesus is not just a branch of David's family tree; he is the root from which the entire line springs. He is the author of all history, both things past and things to come. Jesus also identifies himself as "the bright morning star," a messianic claim (Numbers 24:17). Jesus is the fulfillment of the messianic promise and the one who first promised a deliverer. When Jesus says he is coming soon, we can believe him.

The Book of Revelation closes with an invitation: "Come." Both the Spirit of God and the church as the bride of Christ call people to come. *Come*, surrender to Christ as Lord. *Come*, and receive forgiveness of your sins. *Come*, and enjoy eternity with God. *Come*, have all your heart-longings satisfied by the thirst-quenching water of the Spirit. *Come*. And let those who hear the message of Revelation join us first in following Christ and then in issuing the invitation. Our world needs Christ's hope, and we are called to proclaim the message: *Come*.

Implications and Actions

Our world can seem like a dark and frightening place. Fear and anger permeate the atmosphere. Many people feel unable to trust the institutions and people who are supposed to keep us safe. And yet Christ offers us hope.

The truths of Revelation remind us that there is a vibrant future for those who trust in Christ. Suffering and evil will not have the last word. Jesus wins, and his victory ushers in all the wonders and blessings of life in the presence of God. That is the certain and sure future for the people of God.

What difference does that future hope make now? For one, we can base our decisions on hope rather than anger and fear. Though we may walk through a season of suffering, we know God controls our future. The certainty of our future hope gives us courage and strength to overcome.

Knowing what God has in store for his people should also encourage evangelism. There is enough room in God's house for all who will come, but we must issue the invitation. Christ offers hope in a hopeless world. Will you call them to come?

Lesson 13: *A New Heaven and a New Earth*

Questions

1. How can we know God's promises are true?

2. Which descriptions of life in eternity resonate most with you? Which do you look forward to most?

3. How can we be part of calling people to come to Jesus?

4. What does it mean to be an overcomer? How can we be overcomers?

5. How should our knowledge of life in eternity affect our lives today? How should our future hope affect our present thinking and decisions?

Notes

1. Mitchell G. Reddish, *Smyth & Helwys Bible Commentary: Revelation* (Macon: Smyth & Helwys, 2001), 403.
2. Brian B Blount, *Revelation*. (Louisville: Westminster John Knox Press, 2009), 381.
3. Craig S. Keener, *NIV Application Commentary: Revelation* (Grand Rapids: Zondervan, 2000), 489–490.
4. Reddish, 421.
5. Noel Piper, *Faithful Women and Their God* (Wheaton: Crossway Books, 2005). Kindle Edition.

connect 360
ALL THE BIBLE FOR ALL OF LIFE

Our Next New Study
(Available for use beginning December 2016)

On Your Mark: The Gospel in Motion
A STUDY OF THE GOSPEL OF MARK

Lesson 1	Exercising Spiritual Authority	Mark 1:21–39
Lesson 2	Healing and Forgiveness	Mark 2:1–12
Lesson 3	A Case of Mistaken Identity	Mark 3:20–35
Lesson 4	Invading the Darkness	Mark 5:1–20
Lesson 5	Rejection and Replication	Mark 6:1–13
Lesson 6	Outward Piety vs. Inward Purity	Mark 7:1–23
Lesson 7	A Correct Confession and a Scathing Correction	Mark 8:27–9:1
Lesson 8	Overcoming Unbelief	Mark 9:14–29
Lesson 9	Greatness = Sacrifice	Mark 10:32–45
Lesson 10	Symbolic Acts of Judgment	Mark 11:12–33
Lesson 11	Predictions, Promises, and Pride	Mark 14:12–31
Lesson 12	Betrayed, Arrested, and Tried	Mark 14:43–52; 15:1–15
Lesson 13	Death is Defeated!	Mark 15:33–41; 16:1–8
Christmas Lesson	God is with Us!	Matthew 1:1, 17–25

HOW TO ORDER
More Bible Study Materials

It's easy! Just fill in the following information. For additional Bible study materials available both in print and digital versions, see www.baptistwaypress.org, or get a complete order form by calling 1-866-249-1799 or e-mailing baptistway@texasbaptists.org.

Title of item	Price	Quantity	Cost
This Issue			
Terror and Triumph (Revelation)—Study Guide (BWP001222)	$4.25	_____	_____
Terror and Triumph (Revelation)—Large Print Study Guide (BWP001223)	$4.50	_____	_____
Terror and Triumph (Revelation)—Teaching Guide (BWP001224)	$4.95	_____	_____
Additional Issues Available			
Faith > Fear—Study Guide (BWP001217)	$4.25	_____	_____
Faith > Fear—Large Print Study Guide (BWP001218)	$4.50	_____	_____
Faith > Fear—Teaching Guide (BWP001219)	$4.95	_____	_____
Created for Relationships—Study Guide (BWP001197)	$3.95	_____	_____
Created for Relationships—Large Print Study Guide (BWP001198)	$4.25	_____	_____
Created for Relationships—Teaching Guide (BWP001199)	$4.95	_____	_____
14 Habits of Highly Effective Disciples—Study Guide (BWP001177)	$3.95	_____	_____
14 Habits of Highly Effective Disciples—Large Print Study Guide (BWP001178)	$4.25	_____	_____
14 Habits of Highly Effective Disciples—Teaching Guide (BWP001179)	$4.95	_____	_____
Guidance for the Seasons of Life—Study Guide (BWP001157)	$3.95	_____	_____
Guidance for the Seasons of Life—Large Print Study Guide (BWP001158)	$4.25	_____	_____
Guidance for the Seasons of Life—Teaching Guide (BWP001159)	$4.95	_____	_____
Old Testament			
Exodus: Liberated for Life in Covenant with God—Study Guide (BWP001192)	$3.95	_____	_____
Exodus: Liberated for Life in Covenant with God—Large Print Study Guide (BWP001193)	$4.25	_____	_____
Exodus: Liberated for Life in Covenant with God—Teaching Guide (BWP001194)	$4.95	_____	_____
Choices and Consequences (Joshua/Judges)—Study Guide (BWP001212)	$4.25	_____	_____
Choices and Consequences (Joshua/Judges)—Large Print Study Guide (BWP001213)	$4.50	_____	_____
Choices and Consequences (Joshua/Judges)—Teaching Guide (BWP001214)	$4.95	_____	_____
Psalms: Songs from the Heart of Faith—Study Guide (BWP001152)	$3.95	_____	_____
Psalms: Songs from the Heart of Faith—Large Print Study Guide (BWP001153)	$4.25	_____	_____
Psalms: Songs from the Heart of Faith—Teaching Guide (BWP001154)	$4.95	_____	_____
Jeremiah and Ezekiel: Prophets of Judgment and Hope—Study Guide (BWP001172)	$3.95	_____	_____
Jeremiah and Ezekiel: Prophets of Judgment and Hope—Large Print Study Guide (BWP001173)	$4.25	_____	_____
Jeremiah and Ezekiel: Prophets of Judgment and Hope—Teaching Guide (BWP001174)	$4.95	_____	_____
New Testament			
Jesus: King or Concierge? (Matthew)—Study Guide (BWP001207)	$4.25	_____	_____
Jesus: King or Concierge? (Matthew)—Large Print Study Guide (BWP001208)	$4.50	_____	_____
Jesus: King or Concierge? (Matthew)—Teaching Guide (BWP001209)	$4.95	_____	_____
The Gospel of Mark: People Responding to Jesus—Study Guide (BWP001147)	$3.95	_____	_____
The Gospel of Mark: People Responding to Jesus—Large Print Study Guide (BWP001148)	$4.25	_____	_____
The Gospel of Mark: People Responding to Jesus—Teaching Guide (BWP001149)	$4.95	_____	_____
The Gospel of Luke: Jesus' Personal Touch—Study Guide (BWP001167)	$3.95	_____	_____
The Gospel of Luke: Jesus' Personal Touch—Large Print Study Guide (BWP001168)	$4.25	_____	_____
The Gospel of Luke: Jesus' Personal Touch—Teaching Guide (BWP001169)	$4.95	_____	_____
The Gospel of John: Believe in Jesus and Live!—Study Guide (BWP001187)	$3.95	_____	_____
The Gospel of John: Believe in Jesus and Live!—Large Print Study Guide (BWP001188)	$4.25	_____	_____
The Gospel of John: Believe in Jesus and Live!—Teaching Guide (BWP001189)	$4.95	_____	_____

The Book of Acts: Time to Act on Acts 1:8—Study Guide (BWP001142)	$3.95	_____ _____
The Book of Acts: Time to Act on Acts 1:8—Large Print Study Guide (BWP001143)	$4.25	_____ _____
The Book of Acts: Time to Act on Acts 1:8—Teaching Guide (BWP001144)	$4.95	_____ _____
Romans: A Gospel-Centered Worldview—Study Guide (BWP001202)	$4.25	_____ _____
Romans: A Gospel-Centered Worldview—Large Print Study Guide (BWP001203)	$4.50	_____ _____
Romans: A Gospel-Centered Worldview—Teaching Guide (BWP001204)	$4.95	_____ _____
Letters to the Ephesians and Timothy—Study Guide (BWP001182)	$3.95	_____ _____
Letters to the Ephesians and Timothy—Large Print Study Guide (BWP001183)	$4.25	_____ _____
Letters to the Ephesians and Timothy—Teaching Guide (BWP001184)	$4.95	_____ _____
Hebrews and the Letters of Peter—Study Guide (BWP001162)	$3.95	_____ _____
Hebrews and the Letters of Peter—Large Print Study Guide (BWP001163)	$4.25	_____ _____
Hebrews and the Letters of Peter—Teaching Guide (BWP001164)	$4.95	_____ _____

Coming for use beginning December 2016

On Your Mark: The Gospel in Motion (Mark)—Study Guide (BWP001227)	$4.25	_____ _____
On Your Mark: The Gospel in Motion (Mark)—Large Print Study Guide (BWP001228)	$4.50	_____ _____
On Your Mark: The Gospel in Motion (Mark)—Teaching Guide (BWP001229)	$4.95	_____ _____

Standard (UPS/Mail) Shipping Charges*

Order Value	Shipping charge**	Order Value	Shipping charge**
$.01–$9.99	$6.50	$160.00–$199.99	$24.00
$10.00–$19.99	$8.50	$200.00–$249.99	$28.00
$20.00–$39.99	$9.50	$250.00–$299.99	$30.00
$40.00–$59.99	$10.50	$300.00–$349.99	$34.00
$60.00–$79.99	$11.50	$350.00–$399.99	$42.00
$80.00–$99.99	$12.50	$400.00–$499.99	$50.00
$100.00–$129.99	$15.00	$500.00–$599.99	$60.00
$130.00–$159.99	$20.00	$600.00–$799.99	$72.00**

Cost of items (Order value) _____

Shipping charges (see chart*) _____

TOTAL _____

*Please call 1-866-249-1799 if the exact amount is needed prior to ordering.

**For order values $800.00 and above, please call 1-866-249-1799 or check www.baptistwaypress.org

Please allow two weeks for standard delivery.
For express shipping service: Call 1-866-249-1799 for information on additional charges.

YOUR NAME   PHONE

YOUR CHURCH   DATE ORDERED

SHIPPING ADDRESS

CITY   STATE   ZIP CODE

E-MAIL

MAIL this form with your check for the total amount to:
BAPTISTWAY PRESS, Baptist General Convention of Texas,
7557 Rambler Road, Suite 1200, Dallas, TX 75231–2388
(Make checks to "BaptistWay Press")

OR, **CALL** your order toll-free: 1-866-249-1799
(M-Fri 8:30 a.m.-5:00 p.m. central time).

OR, **E-MAIL** your order to: baptistway@texasbaptists.org.

OR, **ORDER ONLINE** at www.baptistwaypress.org.
(BE SURE TO VISIT OUR NEW WEBSITE)

We look forward to receiving your order! Thank you!